A Dog's History of the World

A Dog's History of the World

*Canines and the Domestication
of Humans*

Laura Hobgood-Oster

BAYLOR UNIVERSITY PRESS

Cover design: *the*BookDesigners
Cover image ©Shutterstock/Frank Lloyd
Book design: Diane Smith

Library of Congress Cataloging-in-Publication Data

Hobgood-Oster, Laura, 1964–
A dog's history of the world : canines and the
domestication of humans / Laura Hobgood-Oster.
 200 pages cm
 Includes bibliographical references and index.
 ISBN 978-1-4813-0019-3 (hardback : alk. paper)
 1. Dogs. 2. Dogs—History. 3. Dog owners. 4. Human-
animal relationships. I. Title.
 SF426.2.H56 2014
 636.7—dc23
                                2013023938

Printed in the United States of America on acid-free paper
with a minimum of 30% post-consumer waste recycled
content.

To Jack, my best friend and conversation partner, who not only puts up with me and all of the dogs who come and go, but is incredibly generous, loving, and supportive in everything we do.

Contents

Acknowledgments

There are so many conversation partners, walking buddies, and inspirations behind this book, I find it hard to know where to begin. But it seems most appropriate to thank the dogs who have lived with me since the day I was born. Of course, the dogs who shared our home as part of our family from my childhood through, now, my middle age, provide a constant source of joy. Also important to note is the endless wisdom I gain from dogs who are homeless, but who never stop trying to find that person who will finally give them a place to live, forever. While writing this book, the dogs from the Williamson County Regional Animal Shelter and from Georgetown Animal Outreach, both in central Texas, have been those constant companions. I must acknowledge the dogs who have found happy endings and those to whom we have gently bid farewell because no human ever took them home.

Also, a huge debt is owed to the staff and volunteers of both those organizations—WCRAS and GAO—who work with dog rescue groups throughout central Texas. Individuals who remind me day-in and day-out that dogs are worth every mile driven and every tear shed: Jimmy Smith, Beth Kosar, Debbie and Dave Frase, Bruce Turbeville, Sheri Biggs, Jeni Williams, Miguel daCunha, Brenda Haile, Cheryl Schneider, Barbara Dunn, Mylissa Waltman, Carol Knight, Jennifer Jurgens, Peggy Goulding, Greg Cunningham, Kira McEntire, Carla Sterner, Misty Valenta, Pamela Morgan, Cherilyn Hack, Debbie Purcell, Tara Stermer, Karen Kroyer, Becky Preston. And to the veterinarians at Koy Animal Hospital for still smiling when I walk in with yet another rescue dog who needs medical attention. Thank you all for your never-ending commitment.

The students, staff, and faculty of Southwestern University continue to make a huge difference both in the classroom and in the world. Special thanks to my colleagues Elaine Craddock, Melissa Johnson, Jimmy Smith, and Romi Burks for their insights into my scholarship and for the many things I learn from them. Students in the "Critical Animal Studies" Paideia cohort, as well as students in the "Animals and Religion" and "Going to the Dogs" courses, have listened to my dog tales for years, helping me to rethink and refine them. And to the broader scholarly community working relentlessly to bring animals into the academy: Paul Waldau, David Aftandilian, Aaron Gross, Donna Haraway, Sid Brown, Jay McDaniel, Marc Bekoff, Anna Peterson. Special thanks to the Brown Foundation as well for supplying research funds through the endowed chair I hold at Southwestern University.

Without the constant, brilliant assistance from Baylor University Press, most particularly Carey Newman, this book probably would never have been completed. I appreciate the consistent reminder that it was worth writing.

My family shares a love of dogs, and I think from the time I was a child it was simply a given that dogs mattered and were part of our family. I am completely indebted to my parents (Chris and Cary Meade), my sister (Cary Lou), my brother (Ben), my nephews (Waylon and Johnny)—all dog (and cat) whisperers in their own ways. And to Jack, to whom this book is dedicated, and our dogs Codi and Cooper—thank you for sticking with me on those late nights when I was sitting writing at the computer instead of sleeping next to all three of you.

Introduction

Laika's early days were spent as a stray dog on the streets of Moscow at the beginning of the Cold War. Her life took an interesting turn one day when she was picked up off the streets. That moment destined her to become a legend—and a hero. Because scientists in the Soviet space program thought that stray dogs, who had endured the hardships of the cold, harsh streets of Moscow would be well-suited to train for space travel, Laika was rescued from the streets. She was taken in from the cold and landed a spot as one of several dogs trained as potential cosmonauts. Laika's story started to look like a rags-to-riches tale—Soviet street dog becomes a hero! Laika had been saved.

But the Soviet space training regimen likely made the cruel streets of Moscow seem like paradise to Laika and the other dogs in the program. They endured day after day in increasingly small compartments to acclimate them to the size of the space capsule. Eventually the dogs even stopped urinating and defecating because the spaces were so tight and uncomfortable. But Laika survived and something about her made the scientists think that she was the one they should use in this massive and public experiment. No earthling had circled the planet before, and the Soviets were determined to get a living animal into orbit.

After placing monitors on her body and strapping her into a small capsule, the little three-year-old mutt shot off into immortality on November 3, 1957. That was also the day of her death. Almost immediately, some of the temperature control systems, as well as the thermal insulation on the space capsule, were compromised so the temperature rose to 104 degrees Fahrenheit. Between the stress of the launch and the rising temperature, Laika's pulse rate increased dramatically, though it finally did settle back down a few hours later. Still, somewhere between five and seven hours after lift-off, no more signs of life were detected in Sputnik 2. Laika was dead. But before she expired, this little street dog from Moscow became the first animal to orbit the earth—preparing the way for many humans to follow her into that final frontier.

Giant steps, like the rocket blast from earth into space, often accompanied by tragic moments such as the death of the canine cosmonaut Laika, mark the human story. After centuries, even millennia, of surviving as small tribes of hunter-gatherers, human groups developed intriguing cultural and religious systems that radically transformed society. Eventually the human shift to controlled plant cultivation—agriculture—and controlled animal cultivation—domestication—changed the entire fabric of human life. After millennia, humans gathered in urban centers that fostered intellectual growth and diversity.[1] An amazing series of feats, but none of these would have been accomplished without the assistance of a good friend.

For over 30,000 years the lives of humans and dogs have been inextricably intertwined. These two species have traveled the world, and beyond, on an emotional, interesting, sometimes beautiful, and at other times destructive, journey. Neither humans, as they currently exist, nor dogs would be here without each other. This pervasive and complicated interspecies connection reminds humans that they are not alone on this journey—and that they could not have walked it without a partner. Because of that powerful and humbling reality, humans are well served by recollecting this story. Without animals in their midst, humans could not have survived. Without dogs in their midst, humans might not exist at all.

As humans morphed into religious and cultural beings, dogs did so as well. These canines are buried alongside humans who are grappling with ideas about the afterlife—ideas that would become "religion." After generations of hunting and gathering, humans domesticated such animals as sheep and pigs in order to have access to reliable food sources. Dogs were the first ones to herd the wild sheep and boars into groups: they made domestication possible. And when humans gathered in large, and disease-filled, centers, certain dogs recaptured their drive to catch prey in order to kill rising populations of rodents, and dogs refined their scavenger skills to dispose of garbage. Humans have leapt over hurdles, but dogs were there to give them a boost.

A journey into the history of this interspecies relationship offers a glimpse into who humans and dogs are, who they have been, and maybe where they might go together. It is not always an easy story. While there are touching moments of companionship, there are also instances of violence and exploitation. But as a team, humans and dogs have dominated earth. Five hundred years ago, the only common animal species known to humans on every inhabited continent was the dog. Dogs had hauled humans into the Arctic, hunted with humans through the last Ice Age so both species could survive that climatic upheaval, and fought beside humans in episodes of war. But dogs have also sat next to humans who were mourning and helped to heal those who suffered. Dogs were tools, but they were also companions.

Almost 2,000 years before Laika soared, literally, into the heavens, humans sent another dog on a journey into the afterlife. A Roman-era cemetery in Carthage offers up a story of human-canine companionship in the form of an intimate burial. A grave unearthed there by archaeologists reveals a young human female with a small dog buried at her feet. While the human obviously experienced an untimely death, the little dog, who was interred with a small bowl next to her head, had lived a long and pampered life. Estimates are that this little Pomeranian or Maltese-like dog—so a lapdog— lived into her late teens. She did suffer from arthritis and tooth decay, indicating that she must have been hand-fed soft foods and carried around, so someone had carefully cared for her. When the life of the young woman came to an end, the apparently beloved dog, spoiled and tenderly attended, joined her in their final, mutual rest.

In the twenty-first century, dogs continue to change who they are because humans change who they are. Dogs exist in an ever-morphing relationship with humans. Maybe humans also exist only in an ever-morphing relationship with dogs? Or, at the very least, humans can only really understand themselves when looking in a mirror that is smudged by a dog's tongue.

Chapter 1

- - - - - - - - -

Strangers No More
Partners in the Hunt and Herd

*To me it is a strangely appealing and even elevating
thought that the age-old covenant between man and dog
was "signed" voluntarily and without obligation by each
of the contracting parties.*

—*Konrad Lorenz*[1]

Over 26,000 years ago, in the deep, damp darkness of a cave
in southwestern Europe, a human child and a canine walked
side by side. The child's torch brushed up against the wall
numerous times, providing a time signature; and their feet
left a 150-foot-long trail that marks the journey they took
together. The archaeological discovery of the footprints of the
young human and the wolf-dog[2] offers a compelling snap-
shot of the beginnings of a story of two species whose lives
would be intertwined for thousands of years to come. This
early human-canine connection evolved into a relationship
through which each species transformed the other in ways
neither could have imagined. It was and is a relationship that
changed the world.

5

La Grotte Chauvet, or Chauvet Cave, where these footprints are preserved, is in the southern Ardèche region of
France and contains art dating back at least 34,000 years.[3]
Considered an archaeological gold mine, the cave's walls are
adorned with hundreds of paintings of animals, including
horses, bison, owls, rhinoceroses, and lions. While it contains
no images of either wolves or dogs, the footprints left by this
child and wolf-dog paint an intriguing portrait. The child
was walking beside his canine companion, not fleeing this
carnivorous hunter. The proto-dog was neither running from
nor toward the child, but accompanied him as they ventured
into the dark cave. They were not enemies: they were friends.
This footprint trail provides a glimpse into the initial stages
of the human-dog partnership.[4] In addition to the footprint
evidence, the cave contained two ancient canid (likely wolf)
skulls, an indication that canines might have been viewed as
sacred or at least powerful in some way.[5] And the information found in Chauvet Cave is not the only archaeological
evidence that pushes the human-dog relationship thousands
of years in advance of the previously assumed scholarly consensus. Additional signs that point to a more complex and
longer-standing human-dog relationship are being discovered
with increasing frequency.[6]

The dog, humankind's "best friend," is unarguably the
first domesticated animal. Indeed the very being named
"dog" delineates this human-connected animal from wolves
(who are not domesticated). Archaeological evidence of the
human-dog relationship is solid starting 15,000 years ago;
from that point forward, the evidence abounds that canines
who were differentiated from wolves were living in close
proximity to and in a special affiliation with humans. But
recently, intriguing, though sporadic, evidence, such as the
Chauvet Cave footprints, has been found that pushes the
existence of dogs back before, or at least contemporaneous

Figure 1
The idea of a child and a dog accompanying each other continues in
cultural representations. This stone relief of a young boy with a dog
was found in the excavation of Pompeii. It was buried when Mount
Vesuvius erupted in 79 CE. Photo by the author.

with, the Last Glacial Maximum (the last "Ice Age"), which started about 26,500 years ago. While some newly developed genetic evidence indicates the possibility of dogs existing over 100,000 years ago, those odds are tenuous.[7]

There are a variety of reasons why it is so problematic to date and locate geographically the first actual, or at least generally accepted, dog. Zooarchaeologists and geneticists are making fascinating progress as they examine ancient remains and study DNA from dogs and wolves all over the globe,[8] but it seems increasingly obvious that there were generations of proto-dog (wolf-becoming-dog) canines living with humans.[9] These proto-dogs became domesticated dogs, possibly fairly

rapidly through an evolutionary process that was also anthropogenic, thus shifting physically and behaviorally. The morphological similarities between dogs and wolves, particularly
at what must have been the earliest stages of their distinction from each other, make it difficult to determine which
archaeological remains mark the beginnings of the process
that culminated in domestication and which, if any, mark its
conclusion.[10]

It is difficult to determine when a group of animals (in this
case the earliest or proto-dogs) finally separates from its wild
ancestor (in this case wolves). While most domesticated animals (cattle, sheep, goats) followed a somewhat more discrete
pattern, one determined more intentionally by humans (and in
some cases shaped by humans along with their dog partners),
proto-dogs likely spent generations betwixt and between their
eventual domesticated forms and wolves. Early on dogs likely
lived in relative isolation from their wild siblings, then rejoined
the wolf packs for centuries, if not millennia, before pairing
up with humans and isolating from wolves again. Such is the
problematic nature of deciding whether bones discovered in
archaeological research are those of wolves or dogs; the remains
are in the morphological canine gray area. Changes in populations of wolves in the process of becoming proto-dogs did not
necessarily lead to speciation, though evolution was, as it still
is, shape-shifting the canines. Another important factor in this
story is that wolves in different parts of the world range in
size dramatically, from about 50 to 175 pounds. Wolf appearance varies dramatically as well. Even the coloring of wolves
ranges significantly—from solid white coats in the Arctic to
gray (interspersed with brown or black) to solid black. This
genetic diversity and interesting suite of factors combine to
give dogs an amazingly diverse genetic inheritance.

As if another interesting twist were needed in this fascinating tale of wolves becoming dogs in the company of humans,

it is highly likely they were semi-domesticated more than once, in sundry places and at different times. Scattered canine remains dating from the period between 26,000 and 30,000 years ago and located in several distinct and geographically remote locations point to the existence of proto-dogs. Some are found in western Europe, others in Siberia and surrounding areas. This apparent emergence of very early dogs is followed by a gap of over ten millennia, with no additional, solid evidence indicating the presence of dogs until 15,000 years ago. Suddenly though, at that point, wherever there were gray wolves and humans, there were also morphologically identifiable dogs. These dogs did not simply show up one day: by fifteen millennia ago dogs had lived with humans for generations and in many discrete and widely distributed locations. From East Asia to the Near East to western Europe to far northeast Asia to Siberia, humans and dogs were living together. Taking a short leap, in evolutionary terms certainly, to 12,000 years ago, North America was also populated by humans and dogs. As a matter of fact, when "Old World" (the three contiguous continents of Europe, Asia, Africa) and "New World" (North and South America) peoples encountered each other five centuries ago, dogs were the only shared domesticated species. The issue of the exact timing of domestication will likely always be debated; discovering "the earliest X" in history challenges other researchers to find an even "earlier X," and so it goes.[11] But without a doubt, dogs and humans populated the planet side-by-side, marking their territory and leaving their footprints as they moved.

So, besides being by far the first domesticated animals, there is another seemingly unique aspect of dogs. Generally a species is domesticated in one location by one group of humans, followed by cultural sharing or trading as humans migrated and came into contact with each other. Following this pattern, it would make sense to assume that dogs come from a single instance of domestication after which these dogs moved with humans.[12] But mounting evidence reveals an alternative, and fascinating, possibility. It seems highly likely that in numerous places where humans and wolves were living together following the last Ice Age, pre-dating 15,000 years ago, dogs evolved in what appear to be independent domestication events, or, better stated, independently occurring evolutionary and cultural processes that eventually led to domestication. This "multiple origin of dog domestication theory" is supported by the significant diversity in dogs during the late glacial period.[13] Small dogs can be identified in southwestern Europe, large dogs (almost wolf-sized) in eastern Europe, medium-sized dogs in the Near East.[14]

There were certainly instances when the first generations, and maybe subsequent ones, of proto-dogs and wolves (and later true dogs and wolves) still interbred, making the genetic evidence even more complex. Continued interbreeding and the evolution of dogs from various populations of wolves, themselves quite distinct from each other, led to a varied and malleable new species—*canis familiaris*.[15] With such diverse genetic pools mingling in the DNA of dogs, the possibilities for various sizes and shapes of dogs exploded.

The possibility that the human-dog relationship developed in apparently disconnected communities as wolves and humans lived together over millennia is not only intriguing but begs a much deeper question: What is it about this particular cross-species partnership that is so obviously mutually beneficial that it happened more than once and in more than one place? Most likely, the ties that bound these two species thousands of years ago as they emerged from the cold of the Glacial Maximum were similarities in hunting practices and social organization. As they tracked and killed prey animals, each species found the other one beneficial for survival (though only some wolves would eventually connect that closely to humans). This partnership was an anomaly in the history of human-animal domestication stories. Wolves, who are primarily carnivores and could prey on humans, were not likely subjects for domestication; and humans, large mammals who survived by hunting and gathering, should have been perceived by wolves as too much of a threat for mutual livelihood. Yet, by 15,000 years ago, humans and dogs did find a way, beneficial to each other, to become partners in the hunt and the herd. There are several different paths that might have led to this fascinating partnership.

The Slow, Unintentional Story

The young child and proto-dog companion trekking through the cave in southern France were not the only canine and early human living together over 20,000 years ago. Caves all over the world continue to yield clues about other early dogs. In Belgium, Siberia, and the Ukraine, skulls have been identified recently which are not quite dogs but also are no longer wolves. And they date to near the beginning of the Last Glacial Maximum, which takes the story of the dog-human relationship down a new trail.

Razboinichya Cave, also known as Bandit's Cave, in the Altai Mountains of southern Siberia near Kazakhstan and Mongolia, is full of bones—over 71,000 of them—that tell the stories of generations of animals. Numerous mammals, including foxes, hyenas, wolves, and bears, along with birds and reptiles, found their final resting place here. Small pieces of charcoal and burnt bones indicate that early humans, already skilled at controlling fire, also used the cave for shelter.[16] One of the bones found in this treasure trove was a canid skull, radiocarbon dated to over 33,000 years before the present, before the last Ice Age. When compared to various wolves and some ancient-type dogs, the skull appears to be an "incipient" dog rather than an abnormal wolf.

Far to the west of the Altai Mountains, in modern-day Belgium, another proto-dog ventured into a cave perched above the Samson valley. Goyet Cave was first excavated in the middle of the nineteenth century. Inside were numerous human artifacts from the Aurignacian (45,000–29,000 years ago), Gravettian (29,000–22,000 years ago), and Magdalenian (17,000–11,000 years ago) periods when humans were creating shell necklaces, ivory beads, and bone harpoons.[17] Among the stash in this cave was a fossil canid, though little else was noted about this find when it was initially discovered. But in the last decade a team of researchers from Belgium, Russia, Great Britain, and Germany took on a major archaeological project to make sense of this and other ancient canid fossils. Comparing the Goyet skull to those of a variety of current dog breeds that are classified as ancient because of their genetic composition—for example, chow chows and Siberian huskies—as well as to wolves and large dogs with wolf-size skulls, such as the Tibetan mastiff, it seems quite probable that the skull in Goyet cave belonged to a 31,700-year-old proto-dog. Based on this skull, along with the one found in Siberia and the evidence from Chauvet Cave, we see the likelihood of an earlier date than ever before considered for the emergence of the first wolves adapted to human society.[18] The curtain was being pulled back on the story of the dog, and it was a much older story than anyone had imagined.

There are a variety of reasons why this information was not gathered and interpreted before. Generally, it was due to a lack of interest or at least a different focus by archaeologists—that is, until relatively recently. Archaeologists overlooked canid skulls, not deeming them terribly important. Only in the late twentieth century did zooarchaeologists begin to examine Palaeolithic canid skulls with new eyes. The canid remains had been ignored, possibly packed away in boxes without a second thought. Obviously, the remains thus far identified are still few and far between, though it is quite likely that additional remains will be discovered as the zooarchaeologists continue to delve into dog history.[19] These large proto-dogs might well still be hiding in plain sight, waiting to be found.[20]

While archaeologists can positively identify proto-dogs between 32,000 and 26,000 years ago,[21] no one can say for certain what happened in the historical gap from 26,000 years ago until domesticated dogs appear en masse and widely distributed between 12,000 and 15,000 years ago. Quite possibly there was a species in between wolf and dog— *canis lupus domesticus*—a wolf en route to domestication.[22] It seems that proto-dogs, or wolves in the beginning phases of morphing into dogs, lived in proximity to humans before the last Ice Age and then reappeared in human communities, with an amazing amount of variety and geographic spread, more than 10,000 years later. There are several conceivable explanations for this historical gap.

One potential answer is that evidence placing these early evolving canids in the 10,000-year interruption has simply not yet been identified as such. If so, then the proto-dogs from before the Ice Age might be the ancestors of domesticated dogs, and their remains might still be identified. Some mitochondrial DNA studies, though fairly widely disputed now, do suggest that this could be the case—according to these scientific measures, dogs have been evolving from wolves for over 100,000 years.[23] Thus, the 10,000-year leap may be filled as additional archaeological and even genetic finds are uncovered.[24]

However, another possibility is that none of these proto-wolf-dogs are truly direct ancestors of the domesticated dog. There could have been a stutter-start to the process. Humans and wolves-becoming-dogs lived together, possibly for thousands of years, and then the Ice Age interrupted our *Homo sapiens* and canine patterns. Humans had to travel more extensively to find food as the frigid climate took hold. This lack of stability kept groups of canines from becoming as isolated from each other. Thus the proper conditions for a new form of canine more adapted to a human-influenced ecological niche no longer existed; the potential for speciation was eliminated for a time.[25]

It is evident, though, that by the time the Last Glacial Maximum ended, the world had changed significantly. Neanderthals, who had competed with humans for thousands of years in Europe, had essentially disappeared. Humans had spread to new continents and were about to emerge as the dominant species on the planet.[26] But now this rapidly ascendant species had a partner in the enterprise of domination: dogs. In other words, humans had paired up with canines twice, once with the proto-wolf-dog before the Ice Age and then again after that cataclysmic period ended. The second time, the interspecies marriage would stick.

And there are myriad reasons why these two kindred species would unite (or reunite, as the case may be). The overlapping ecological niches, similar diets, and comparable social hierarchies of humans and canines made this pairing a natural fit. Humans and canines are both opportunistic feeders. Early *Homo sapiens* were hunter-gatherers who moved from place to place in search of their next meal. Wolves, minus the intensive gathering practices, are basically the same. Humans and wolves were hunting many of the same animals, using differing and complementary skills in this pursuit. Wolves were better at tracking by scent and could easily outrun humans; however, humans were developing formidable tools to bring down larger animals. Still, that alone is not a sufficient explanation. Wolves were hardly the only overlapping hunters. Many other large animals were searching for prey and their next meal. Consider, for example, the lions and bears of pre–Ice Age Europe, with whom humans did not develop a partnership. The crucial element that likely came into play is the similar social and hierarchical structure shared by humans and wolves. Wolves live in packs with a definite alpha male and female pair. The rest of the pack has a rigid order that is kept in check by the alpha male; the order changes rarely and, when it does so, only with much drama and some inevitable violence. Humans were able to insert themselves into this order, albeit maybe not deliberately, basically becoming the alpha wolf in the new pack and taking over that position in the dominance hierarchy.

There are very few opportunistic social hunters who do their primary hunting during the day. But both humans and wolves do so. This combination of being a social, or pack, animal and hunting when you can see and be seen made the two species natural cohabitators, sometimes competitors, and, eventually, allies. Then, after this initial overlap of hunting space was reconciled, certain wolves, likely the ones who were not alpha in their own pack, must have discovered that eating the scraps humans threw away, or eating the bones that humans could not eat (figure 2), was an alternative and fairly reliable way to survive. These wolves, having become somewhat accustomed to living around humans, began to live in even closer proximity to them. Their initial instinct to flee from this hominid hunter was overridden by the benefits of the scraps found at the edges of settlements or left behind on the hunting trail. Humans, protecting themselves, would have either scared off or killed the wolves who were particularly threatening.

Eventually these close wolf neighbors who had adapted somewhat to human camps began to breed with each other, thus subverting their previous dominance hierarchy since none of these were alpha wolves (those were the ones who, not really needing to eat from the trash, had chosen to stay away altogether, or whom humans had killed because of their

Figure 2
One of three canid skulls found in the Czech Republic at the
Predmosti site, dating to roughly 31,500 years ago. This particular
skull was buried with a mastodon bone in its mouth. The speci-
men is held at the Moravian Museum (Anthropos Institute at
Brno, Czech Republic). Photo courtesy of Dr. Mietje Germonpré.

aggression). Some wolves found new niches close to humans and decided to live there rather than with their pack because it was a better bet for their own survival.

These wolves, who were less likely to flee from humans, bred and reproduced pups with similar characteristics.[27] The resulting pups were marked by complex and potent hormonal changes, changes that intensified with each successive generation. The transformation from wolf to dog was underway. Over what might have been a relatively few generations in an evolutionary perspective, the wolves-becoming-dogs started to exhibit signs of domestication as the two species bonded and as the hormonal responses of the now increasingly tame wolves made significant alterations. During this time period the proto-dogs' tails began to curl, their coats changed colors, and their ears started to flop. An entire suite of characteristics emerged, and through this process the modern-day dog eventually came into being.[28] Humans no doubt recognized the value of having the proto-dogs around—they alerted them to danger with howls and assisted in hunting with their excellent scenting and running abilities.

This compelling theory of the wolf-becoming-dog through canine initiative warrants further research. An evolutionary process resulting in domestication that was not initiated directly by humans rewrites human history. And if this process of local wolf populations morphing into early domesticated dogs sometime before 15,000 years ago took place through somewhat parallel evolutionary and then cultural processes in Europe, Asia, and possibly northern Africa, then history is again turned on its head. That being the case, dogs are not a "creation" of humans that were then shared through cultural exchange; rather they were natural partners in different times and places who took some of the initiative in this project themselves. Humans did not create dogs through their own intelligence and selection, wolves and dogs were intimately involved in the project.

Around that time, 15,000 years ago, the process was well underway and humans likely became more proactive in selecting for traits that would mark the first true domestication of another animal species. Friendly, or at least less dominant, wolves who sought out the edges of human habitations for food had become constant companions and helpers. Humans, no evolutionary slouches at the time, were already formidable hunters, but dogs added to their toolbox.

There is an additional aspect to this story as well. It is highly likely that humans did affect the process, somewhat unwittingly, in another way. While the wolves who were not alphas and who benefited the most from living in close proximity to humans made one move in the evolutionary dance, humans also made a move by both selecting the most tamable pups and simultaneously chasing off, or even killing, the most aggressive wolves who were approaching the human

fires and hunting parties.[29] By 15,000 years ago, anthropogenic environments—those locations marked by the impact
and continuous presence of human populations—were beginning, unintentionally in most cases, to change the face of the
planet and the other animals in their midst.[30] In a sense, without even knowing what they were doing, wolves and humans
made some evolutionary selections that eventually led to the
dog. Both social hunting groups with a long track record of
survival in an ever-changing world, they were ideal partners.
And humans were not alone in this planet-changing process,
dogs were partnering with them in the transformation.[31] By
that point, the partnership was poised to explode onto the
global scene.

Such a scenario could have happened before the Ice Age
and again after the Ice Age, the second and more profound
round of partnership becoming a permanent and abiding
social relationship that could positively be labeled domestication. In between those two periods, wolves and dogs
continued to share their genes through interbreeding. This
wolf-dog mixture persists into the modern period, providing
a glimpse into the past. As a matter of fact, studies examining the skulls of Siberian huskies who either escaped or
were released as late as the first half of the twentieth century
indicate that these dogs continued to hybridize with Arctic
wolves.[32] These canine populations were not yet different species, but a fluid contingency of wolf-dogs living in and among
humans, some more domesticated than others, then drifting
back into a more wolf-like state. The final speciation—the
dog—finally decided to leave the wolf ancestor behind and
join with this new, seemingly dominant primate by 15,000
years ago, and never intentionally looked back again. Around
that time humans likely became more proactive in selecting
for traits that would mark the first true domestication of a
species other than themselves.

As humans and dogs started to live together, both species' digestive systems took a turn. Recent research comparing dog and wolf DNA indicates clearly that dogs "coevolved with humans and their diet."[33] Domestic dogs eventually adapted to eating starch, just as humans did, thousands of years ago. After the last Ice Age when human populations began to grow and move around again, they also carried with them (unintentionally at first) the fruits and grains they favored. This was the agriculture before agriculture. Human digestive systems morphed as they changed from hunter-gatherer cultures to ones more reliant on agriculture, even in its nascent forms. As dogs started to eat more starchy foods, such as wild rice and grains, from human trash piles, they developed extra copies of a gene (amylase) that enabled them to digest these foods more effectively. Sharing similar environments and food meant that humans and dogs experienced some of the same genetic shifts.[34] This physical change in both species paralleled the cultural change from primarily carnivorous diets to more omnivorous, and starchy, ones.[35]

So, while evidence for the first wave of proto-dog is scarce and still debated, as undoubtedly it will be for years to come, that for the second (and widely accepted) enduring wave of dogs, the first generations of starch-eating ones, abounds. Some of this proof comes from burial sites, with evidence of dog remains intentionally interred by humans tracing back to at least 14,000 years ago.[36] While zooarchaeologists have made solid progress in creating an inventory of these burials, more work is needed before scientists will see with more clarity how the human-dog relationship unfolded.

Long thought to be the most ancient evidence of the domestic dog, a 14,000-year-old canine jawbone was discovered in a grave along with a young woman and an old man close to Bonn, Germany. The "Bonn-Oberkassel dog" held that esteemed position as the first domesticated dog for years, and many archaeologists still identify Bonn-Oberkassel as the oldest solid archaeological evidence of a domesticated dog. It is truly amazing that this intentional burial, in a grave with humans, is where the dog officially begins in the archaeological world.[37] Obviously by this early point dogs already occupied a position in human culture that led to ritual interment: dogs were not a new player in the human drama, but an established and meaningful one. Over the course of thousands of years, wolves had moved in and out of the edges of human cultures, becoming dog-like and then wolf-like again. Lurking in the shadows, then joining a little closer to share the warmth of the fire and the benefit of discarded leftovers. In a move that would end up changing the world, some wolves discovered significant advantages in living close to the interesting primate who tossed a bone their way.

The Rapid, Human-Orchestrated Story

Unique among all domestic animals,
the first unambiguous domestic dogs precede
the appearance of settled agriculture in the archaeological
record by several thousand years.[38]

Domesticating animals is not an easy task. Of the dozens of large mammals that humans might have considered trying to control and reshape to human needs, only fourteen were ever successfully domesticated and only five of those (sheep, goats, cows, pigs, horses) have a widespread impact.[39] Those few who were domesticated share certain traits related to social organization, diet, mating habits, and disposition, among others. This means that most species are not good candidates for domestication. Interestingly, dogs do not fit the model as well as the other five major domesticates, even though dogs were domesticated thousands of years before those other animals and, most likely, aided significantly in the process of harnessing the others.

Some hints as to when and how the final, refining steps of the domestication of dogs happened can be seen in a long-term study of another canine—the silver fox. Over forty years ago in Russia, geneticists began an experiment to test the hypothesis that selecting for behavioral traits in wild animals would also lead to physical and morphological changes—thus resulting in domestication. This research, the ongoing "farm-fox experiment," has been widely studied and summarized.[40] Its conclusions directly impact interpretations of what might have happened thousands of years ago with humans and wolf-dogs.

Vulpes vulpes, the silver fox, was chosen for the study primarily because there were a large number of these animals held in captivity for the fur trade industry. This species is relatively close on the genetic tree to *canis familiaris,* but the silver fox had never been domesticated. The experiment began one step into the domestication process; the thirty male and one hundred female foxes had already been captured, and lived on a fur farm isolated from their wild relatives. The team of researchers then selected for tamability alone, not for physical traits. For example, at the age of one month, a pup was tested to see if she or he would take food from the experimenter's hand. This test was repeated monthly, sometimes when the pups were alone, other times when they were with other pups in order to give them the choice between approaching or avoiding the human. Based on the foxes' response, the experimenters placed them in different groups: those who would flee, those who let themselves be handled but really were not interested in humans, and those who were friendly to humans to the extent of wagging their tails. After six generations of aggressively selecting and breeding the most tamable, the category "domesticated elite" was added. These foxes eagerly sought human companionship, even licking the hands of the experimenters and whining to get their attention.[41]

Amazingly, by selecting just for behavioral traits, certain physical characteristics manifested, as well. The foxes' ears began to flop, their tails curled, their coat became piebald and they exhibited characteristics of neoteny. In other words, they became childlike versions of their wild selves. Other important changes also occurred after many years of the continuing experiment (which is still being carried out by a new generation of scientists). The structure of the skull is beginning to change in the domesticated foxes, as are their reproductive cycles. In short, the stresses of domestication and hormonal changes led to these morphological shifts—the two effects were inextricably intertwined.[42]

Applying this experiment to what might have occurred in the wild thousands of years ago yields fascinating results. As some populations of wolves colonized human-dominated environments, protodomestication started and, with it, hormonal responses to the first stages of domestication. Henceforth, the pivotal human-dog relationship turning point occurred somewhere between 15,000 and 30,000 years ago. Evolution took over, and some wolves began to change behaviorally and, through the related physical outcomes, morphologically—their appearance, size, and demeanor all changed simultaneously. Later in the process, humans became intentionally engaged, and classic domestication, conscious and unconscious human selection, resulted in the dog.[43] It is important to note that the farm-fox experiment was obviously very intentional and forceful with only the most elite foxes selected. Nothing along these lines would have happened with humans and wolves. But the discovery of the hormonal-morphological-domestication triangle sheds significant light on the human selection part of the dog domestication equation.

Over the next fifteen millennia, humans became even more directly involved in the selection process, as is obvious when one looks at dogs today—the most varied species on the planet in terms of the size of an adult animal, with the largest weighing over 250 pounds and the smallest under three pounds.[44] Some are made to dig, others to swim, others to run at amazing speeds, others to sit on laps. With the genetic background of many different kinds of wolves and the eventual selection by humans for diverse roles, the dog became many different dogs.

Making a Killing Together: Humans and Canines in the Hunt . . .

Once again, the history of humans and dogs is uncovered by entering a cave. La Grotte du Lazaret, a "long-term habitation site" for Palaeolithic humans close to modern-day Nice, France, is filled with bones! Over 70,000 remains of various animals were found in this cave, which also housed humans over 125,000 years ago.[45] Inside, these early hunter-gatherers built shelters, brought the catches from their hunts, and carried out what seem to be ritual practices. Intentionally placed at the entrances to the internal shelters are the skulls of wolves.[46]

As is evident from the discussion thus far, theories abound that dogs and humans lived together for lengthy periods of time before humans finally began to settle into less migratory patterns. In other words, we hunted and gathered side-by-side before we set up permanent camp. New evidence of more ancient proto-dogs supports the theory of extending this relationship even further into the past. Evidence from China 500,000 years ago, England 400,000 years ago, and France 150,000 years ago links *Homo erectus* and wolves. Throughout the Northern Hemisphere, literally for hundreds of thousands of years, ancient wolves and humans lived close enough to each other that both species' bones ended up in the same piles after death.[47]

What is obvious, though, is that by the time humans developed more sophisticated hunting weapons over 12,000 years ago, the descendants of some of these ancient wolves, now evolved into dogs, were working closely with humans to stalk and kill more animals than had previously been possible. In a central Russian plain, another collection of bones provides insight into this new hunting pact arranged between humans and early Ice Age dogs. The site, Eliseevichi I, includes deposits as old as 17,000 years. Two adult dog skulls, resembling Siberian huskies but larger, were found here along with large quantities of mammoth bones (including some shaped as figurines). This evidence points to the likelihood that the dogs were intentionally part of the hunt, already partnered with humans in this enterprise of survival in a harsh climate.[48] Of course, the existence of these hunting dogs at that point provides even more evidence for a date earlier than 15,000 years ago for some stage of canine domestication.

Dogs were helping hunt for other animals as well, not just the mammoth, and some of these other animals would eventually join dogs in the category of domesticates. For example, though less frequently on the menu in the twenty-first century, a staple part of the diet for humans in central Europe 13,000 years ago (Magdalenian culture) was the horse. Along with foxes, hares, and reindeer, bones from horses that were hunted and eaten are common archaeological finds in caves and other sites that tell the tale of humans pursuing and consuming these large mammals for generations. As a matter of fact, between 12,000 and 13,000 years ago, at three separate sites in eastern Germany, there is a common denominator: if humans were focused on hunting horses more than other species, evidence of early domesticated dogs exists as well.[49] Possibly, then, at least in this part of the world, humans and dogs take the first steps of domestication in conjunction with what will eventually become the domesticated horse.[50]

This pattern of team hunting was fairly obvious in North America and has been widely accepted by scientists for years. Humans and dogs came into North America together some-time between 14,000 and 12,000 years ago, crossing the Ber-ing land bridge.[51] And, with their new weapons in tow (maybe on sleds pulled by dogs), they began to hunt. At that point, the continent was inhabited by mammoths, mastodons, and giant ground sloths, to name just a few of the large animals who filled the great expanse. Evidence of dog and Palaeo-Indian hunting habits emerges from various archaeological sites throughout the hemisphere. At Blackwater Draw, a Clo-vis "kill site" in New Mexico, the tailbones of mammoth indicate what is known as kennel damage. In other words, around 13,000 years ago early stage domesticated dogs were hanging out with humans when the mammoth carcasses were processed and were chewing on the bones.[52] Just as is the case in many kitchens today, whoever was working on dinner tossed a few bones for the dogs to eat. Similar findings at sites in Arizona and, later, at Fell's Cave in South America show the same kennel damage on bones, likely caused by small, and still somewhat wolf-like, dogs.[53] By some accounts, 11,000 years ago the megafauna of North America were being hunted to extinction by humans and their dogs, who had recently arrived together in this new ecosystem. Called the "Pleistocene overkill," or black hole hypothesis in North America, it suggests that human-dog hunting teams were a formidable force.[54]

The hunting pattern repeats itself over and over again. When dogs arrived in Japan almost 10,000 years ago (dur-ing the Jomon period which dates from 10,000–400 BCE), hunting was still the norm. These ancient Jomon dogs likely migrated from mainland Asia and are probably the ances-tors of modern-day shiba-type dogs. Numerous archaeo-logical sites include remains of Jomon period dogs, and their characteristics continued in a fairly stable state for thousands of years. Then, when rice agriculture was introduced to Japan just over 2,000 years ago and hunting became less important, dogs became less valuable as hunting companions. Evidence reflects this cultural shift as dogs found in archaeological sites decline sharply at that point.[55] This might be one area where, for some reason, dogs did not adapt as quickly, either physically or culturally, to the change from a hunting-based to a starch-based diet.

Dogs as hunting companions are not only the stuff of the practical, everyday survival for humans, dogs also become the stuff of image, myth, and legend involving the hunt. In the Acacus Mountains of Libya they are portrayed aiding in the hunt in rock art images dating between 7,000 and 3,000 years ago.[56] Later, in Egypt, the land of the hunting sight hounds, they are depicted in fabulous images and even as children's toys. One fascinating example is a 3,500-year-old "leaping hunting dog" carved from ivory; the dog's mouth can be opened and closed with a lever to reveal teeth and a red tongue.[57]

It is fitting then, that the brightest object in the sky (after the sun and moon) is Sirius, who, according to Greek mythology, is a hunting dog following his master, Orion. After Orion was plucked from the earth and placed in the sky, his dog searched endlessly for him. Finally, Artemis, the Greek goddess of the hunt whose temples often included dogs and who was frequently accompanied by dogs in her own iconography, took pity on Sirius and placed him in the sky with Orion. There the dog and the human hunt together for eternity. It is an appropriate myth and a nightly reminder that these two species started their millennia-old bond as partners in the hunt.

. . . *and in the Herd*

More ancient rock carvings tell stories of humans, dogs, and other animals negotiating life together in these bygone eras.

Some sites with these ancient carvings that have just recently been examined fully are in the mountains of Armenia. Here there are 5,000-year-old images of humans herding with dogs and hunting for goats (one of the first animals domesticated after the dog, probably around 10,000 years ago).[58] A site in Egypt yields equally revealing tales in rock art from approximately 3,200 BCE. Images of humans and dogs hunting bulls, including a compelling image of a dog standing on top of a cow or bull, indicating the dog was in control of the larger animal, suggest a joint effort to dominate the bovine.[59] This depiction fits well with estimates that cows were first domesticated around 6,000 years ago in several different places, including North Africa. Further east on the steppes of Asia, in present-day Kazakhstan, the ancient Botai people relied on thick-coated, Samoyed-like dogs to herd horses. From as early as 3,300 BCE, this fairly specific dog type (if not quite a breed), the Botai dog, is identifiable and central to this particular human culture. As a matter of fact, Botai dogs still hunt alongside horses and humans today.[60]

Starting about 10,000 years ago, across the Eurasian landmass a few large mammals joined the human-dog household. At first there were just three additional species—sheep, goats, and pigs. Later cows, horses, donkeys, and water buffalo would follow. There are actually amazingly few large domesticated mammals, all things considered. As mentioned above, out of almost one hundred and fifty such species, only fourteen were domesticated, and for all of these the process took place sometime between 8,000 and 2,500 years ago.[61] Just as the social structure of wolves blended well with that of humans in the hunt, the social structure of these fourteen species allowed them to be herded more easily. Because individuals in these species are tolerant of each other, they bunch up in groups. Herds of sheep and goats live together, huddling in a crowd for safety. With this pattern already in place, humans and their hunting partners, the dogs, worked together to gather these animals in manageable groups—thus providing ready access to reliable animal products for food, clothing, and tools. Just as plant agriculture allowed for a more controlled and dependable diet, domesticating and herding the few other animals with the appropriate traits provided consistent access to these necessary resources.

Dogs and Humans Become Domesticated

From at least 15,000 years ago onward, then, dogs become partners in hunting, herding, and, more broadly, in the morphing of culture generally. In some places, depending on climate and varying conditions, they provide other support—such as hauling humans and their belongings. They shape-shift with amazing speed from about 5,000 years ago forward, adapting to changing human-influenced environments and to the myriad ecosystems into which early humans began to spread. While fascinating morphological and physiological shifts are observed in other animals that have undergone the process of domestication, none are as dramatic as those that eventually take place in dogs.

A recent study of prehistoric Italian dogs sheds light on this transformation. The study examined over two thousand specimens from domesticated dogs recovered from excavations in Italy dating from 8,000 years ago to the end of the Roman period, the sixth century CE. At the beginning of the period, dogs were close in size to the modern day dingo. But very quickly, though likely the result of accidental crossbreeding, the Bronze Age (4,000 years ago) ushers in dogs who are similar to modern dachshunds, followed by dogs who have long muzzles, similar to the greyhound. It took centuries for very large dogs, such as mastiffs, and very small lapdogs to appear, but some amazing variety, only possible through human intervention, did take place relatively early in the increasingly heavily human-populated Mediterranean world.[62] Humans had started the process that eventually led to the most varied species on Earth—dogs.

Interestingly, in many of the places where evidence of ancient dogs is found, there are three or four distinctly different sizes of dogs. In caves in Armenia, for example, rock carvings of dogs, dating from the third to the first millennium BCE, show three dog shapes that are repeated consistently: one with a short straight tail that resembles a sheepdog, another with cocked ears and a curled tail that looks like a Siberian husky, and a third that resembles an Armenian greyhound. People were already using specific dogs for specific tasks—some for hunting, others for guarding livestock, others for guarding homes, and maybe already some for pure companionship.[63]

Similarly in North and South America, aboriginal dogs (who are most likely descendant from Eurasian wolves) fall into three basic breeds, from a large Eskimo-type dog with a wolf-like appearance (a broad muzzle, though smaller than the gray wolf typical of the same area) to the slightly smaller Plains Indian dogs, and finally to the smallest type of dogs who were similar to little terriers.[64] And in Mexico, before the Spanish conquests, four definitive forms of dogs, including a rare hairless dog (Xoloitzcuintli) and a small companion-sized dog, show up in the archaeological records.[65] The archaeological remains for all of these American dogs are still being examined, and there is much left to learn.[66]

Amazingly similar human needs paired with the malleable, globally present dog led to somewhat similar selection even in these earliest attempts to control dog size, shape, and purpose. Other species also live in common with humans as they rapidly inhabit a larger portion of the earth and become increasingly sedentary. One common outcome of this process of domestication is a smaller body size for other animals when they start to live with humans. For example, sheep, cattle, and pigs are all smaller in their domesticated form than their wild ancestors.[67] There will be a few interesting exceptions to this, notably in the eventual selective breeding of dogs.[68] But dogs are the first and foremost species with whom humans try out the possibility of domestication, and they quickly become an indicator of the incredible shifts to come.

What of the Puppy Phenomenon?

Infants of many species are appealing, few more so than puppies. For years theories about dog domestication revolved around the idea that children and women in hunting-gathering cultures adopted abandoned or orphaned wolf puppies, took them home, and, basically, domesticated them. Elizabeth Thurston, a historian of companion animals, suggests that "prehistoric women might have been primarily responsible for forging the first intimate relationships with canids."[69] While this theory has a certain appeal, there also seem to be gaps in it. First, as the wolf puppy grew up, she or he would become increasingly unwieldy and, likely, too rough to be kept in a human camp. Second, at the time period in question, thousands of years ago, cages or ropes that would secure an animal with the strength of a wolf were simply not yet part of the human toolbox. So as a theory of the mass domestication of dogs, the process of adopting individual wolf puppies is highly unlikely.

But, did caretakers for those who were ailing, likely women in these nomadic or barely settled groups, find a baby wolf, take the pup home, and use him to relieve stress and anxiety? Or after the loss of a human child, did grieving mothers reach out to other infants in order to fill a void? Could a child find an orphaned wolf puppy and take her home as a pet, albeit for a relatively short period of time until she was too strong to handle? All of these scenarios are highly likely and probably did contribute, in the long run, to some aspect of domestication. Certainly, by the time that wolves were becoming dogs (the "proto-dog") and living in close proximity to humans, a more direct intervention based on the puppy theory is much more probable. At that point the increasingly tame puppies could more easily have been hand-reared by humans.

One window into this possible scenario is the clear evidence that many groups of dogs in the modern period live in between tame and wild—the Australian dingo, Indian pariah, and New Guinea singing dogs are prime examples. These canines who exist on the edges of human culture are still often redomesticated or readapted in succeeding generations. Already accustomed to living in and around humans, but not in the very direct relationship of a constant companion or pet, the tamer ones are incorporated into daily life. For thousands of years a similar pattern may have repeated itself globally as dogs became dogs.

Another interesting hint from the children–women–puppies–dogs relationship is the role of breastfeeding. The practice of women breastfeeding puppies has been documented in at least four different cultural settings—Copper Inuit (Canada), Aranda (Australia), Yanomamo (Venezuelan and Brazilian Amazon), and Andamanese (Bay of Bengal).[70] It is possible that this practice was much more widespread, with some evidence of women nursing puppies in European and other North American cultures also. There are thus some definite hints that make quite probable the role of women, specifically, as caretakers of puppies and agents in domestication.

Entering the Future Together

Images of Romulus and Remus, the mythological twin brothers who founded the city of Rome, abound in that ancient metropolis. But they are not alone in these icons: the two little boys are being suckled by a female canine. Tradition calls her a "she-wolf," but the earliest depiction, the Capitoline Wolf, which is reproduced endlessly, is decidedly dog-like with a shorter nose and more defined forehead. The two boys hang on her, and, through her adoption and care of them, she literally guarantees that Rome (and later its Empire) will emerge. Such stories of the founding of human culture are naturally intertwined with canines.

Whether the journey together started 15,000 years ago or 30,000 years ago will remain an active and intriguing question. But as more and more pieces of the puzzle fit together, the coevolution picture becomes increasingly clear. As Ice Age hunters preyed on the same animals and organized groups in similar ways, humans and dogs formed a unique and powerful bond. And, eventually as a result, in every part of the world inhabited by humans, there are dogs.[71]

Chapter 2

- - - - - - - - -

Journey to the Afterlife
Best Friends Forever

Figure 3
A memorial marker at Hartsdale Pet Cemetery, the oldest official cemetery for pets in the United States. Photo courtesy of Hartsdale Pet Cemetery and historian Mary Thurston.

A Tribute to a Best Friend

Sunlight streams through window pane
unto a spot on the floor . . .
then I remember,
it's where you used to lie,
but now you are no more . . .
It's where your paws would joyously bound . . .
But I'll take that vacant spot of floor
and empty muted hall
and lay them with the absent voice
and unused dish by the wall.
I'll wrap these treasured memorials
in a blanket of my love
and keep them for my best friend
until we meet above.

—Author unknown[1]

A large corner cabinet, carefully dusted and arranged, announced the centrality of dogs to this modest stone home in central Texas. The humans living here, a couple in their early sixties, spoiled and pampered the dogs. After lives of cuddling and napping on laps, when the time came for each dog to bid a final farewell, she or he had a new spot designated in the cabinet. The day I visited there were already fifteen small urns, each with a picture, name and the arrival and departure dates of a precious Chihuahua. In addition to the tiny dogs who had already taken their supposed, or at least hopeful, journey to the afterlife, the five current pet Chihuahuas bounced happily around the house. This was Chihuahua heaven while the dogs were alive and, based on the status of those in the memorial corner, the humans hoped for Chihuahua paradise after their death.

Thousands of generations ago humans and dogs paired up with each other. From the beginning the relationship has been more than pragmatic. Depths of meaning lie beneath the surface and, at times, come bubbling up, revealing something of the primal essence of this interspecies partnership. As humans started to ask questions about what matters, about why some live and others die, about suffering and love, dogs were already lurking in our shadows and in our memories. These are all religious questions—these deep questions of meaning. To understand truly the dog-human journey, its religious nature must be acknowledged and comprehended.

Even acknowledging that other animals have something to do with the religious foundations and sensibilities of humans can be a controversial claim. But prehistoric expressions of a quest for meaning frequently include other animals. Cave paintings, such as those in Chauvet, beg for interpretation as nascent religious texts. While the actual reason or reasons that *Homo sapiens* also became *Homo religiosus* may never be known, there is one widely dreaded tragedy of life that has certainly sent humans on a quest for understanding—death. And in this hunt to figure out why humans die, they often sought the company of dogs.

From all appearances, or at least as far as the popular media covers phenomena, the last twenty years have witnessed the growth of a new "craze"—formal rituals for interring or at least memorializing dogs.[2] But delving deeper sheds a different light on this apparent trend. Humans and dogs share intimate and forceful connections in life. But in addition to that powerful link, for thousands of years these two companion species have been bound together by and in death. So, while this connection to dogs as significant subjects in the quest to comprehend or grapple with death might seem to be a relatively new, albeit powerful, religious phenomenon, deep historical roots provide insight into the long-standing relationship between humans, dogs, and their shared experiences of death, as well as their journeys into the afterlife. Interestingly, some of the earliest hints of the human-dog shared living spaces are their dying places. Incidents of common interment, the joint ritual burial of humans and dogs, show up early in the archaeological record. Delving into this fascinating history of the dog's journey into the afterlife, or at least the human speculation about this hoped for canine eternity, provides yet another window into the significance of this cross-species bond.

Something Old or Something New?

Alas Poor Zoe.
Born October 1st. 1879.
Died August 13th. 1892.
As deeply mourned as ever dog was mourned.[3]

Commemorating and ritualizing the dog dead stretches back thousands of years. But relatively recently, during the Victorian Age in England, a vivid imagination of death merged with the rapidly growing idea of canine fidelity to generate a new focus on dog memorials.[4] It was in this era, a type of golden age for many pet dogs, that the first modern pet cemetery was founded. Sentimental ideas about death and the afterlife are reflected in passionate and personal dog memorials.[5] The first small pet cemetery was in London's Hyde Park. In 1881 a little Maltese named Cherry, who belonged to frequent visitors at the park, died from old age. The family asked the keeper of the Victoria's Gate Lodge if they, perchance, could bury Cherry in the back garden since the little dog had so loved visiting the park. The gatekeeper gladly agreed and, for the next several decades, pets were interred in this quaint, peaceful cemetery. The headstones clearly indicate a hoped-for afterlife for the beloved canines. Darling "Tiddy" 1895–1901, was remembered with this expectation: "Shall he whose name is love deny our loving friends a home above? Nay, he who orders all things for the best in paradise will surely give them rest." And the headstone for Wee Bobbit, who died in 1901 after six years as a "most devoted friend," reads, "When our lonely lives are o'er and our spirits from this earth shall roam we hope he'll be there waiting to give us a welcome home."[6] Not only a statement of hope, the ideas on these headstones express a plea to the divine, a genuine request to grant a place in heaven for the adored, faithful dogs.[7]

Across the Channel in France, the *Cimetière des Chiens et Autres Animaux Domestiques* (Cemetery of Dogs and Other Domestic Animals) just outside of Paris was also established in the late nineteenth century. At that point a new law had gone into effect in Paris requiring pets to be buried at least 100 meters from the nearest home, rather than either being thrown out with the garbage or clandestinely buried in small yards or plots. Thus the first public dog cemetery in France opened to accommodate the new need for an interment space. Famous dogs, including "Rin Tin Tin," the German shepherd movie star who originally hailed from France during World War I, are buried there, and monuments to dog heroes such as Barry, the Saint Bernard, fill the lawn. Barry's headstone reads, "he saved the lives of forty people, he was killed by the forty-first" (apparently from exhaustion after carrying so many people to safety, not a deliberate attack on the dog hero). This Saint Bernard deserves the title of dog-martyr nonetheless.[8] "Drac," the pet of a Romanian princess (Elisabeth, who married George II, king of Greece, who was later exiled), also graces the lawn and gives us insight into Elisabeth's situation as well, "Fidèle compagnon des heures tragiques; Ami précieux dans l'exil" ("Faithful companion during tragic times and precious friend in exile"). Apparently this Romanian woman found comfort in the fact that Drac (a fitting name for a Romanian hound) accompanied her to her new home. Less prominent canine inhabitants still have elaborate statues, some with framed images of the dog interred below, and touching memorials adorn the headstones. An interesting short tribute film provides a panorama of the graveyard, giving the viewer a sense of the intimacy expressed in these final canine resting places.[9]

The nineteenth-century practice of establishing formal cemeteries for dogs and other pets expanded rapidly to the United States. Hartsdale Pet Cemetery, located just outside of New York City, was founded in 1896 by Dr. Samuel Johnson, a veterinarian who had also been instrumental in establishing the American Society for the Prevention of Cruelty to Animals (figure 3). The cemetery is still functioning and growing over a century later. Almost 70,000 pets (mostly dogs, though also cats, rabbits, and even a lion cub) are buried there.[10] And Hartsdale is definitely not alone. From this same time period, stories of individual dogs and the people who cared about them enough to memorialize them after death are frequently shared.

One example from the opposite side of the United States is Faust, a tough little American water spaniel, who traveled to Alaska with his owner, the equally tough Frances E. "Fizzy" Fitz. Fizzy was one of the few women participating in the Alaskan Gold Rush of the early twentieth century. Images from the time show the two of them trekking through the frontier, mining for gold and surviving in the rough world of the Seward Peninsula in Alaska. As a successful woman living in a difficult and dangerous culture, Fizzy trusted Faust to take on such important roles as safeguarding their earnings. Fizzy kept her savings in a leather pouch on Faust's collar. He had been her companion for sixteen years when he died, and this fact, combined with their rather extraordinary life together, earned him a lengthy obituary in the *Seattle Daily Times* in 1906. The memorial hailed him as "one of the best-known dogs of the Seward Peninsula" and remarked on his "varied and picturesque career." Not only had he traveled "with the luxury of a prima donna over more than 25,000 miles," he was "the only dog ever permitted cabin passage on the steamship Victoria." The remarkable, substantive obituary concluded with an indication of his burial place, the dog cemetery beyond Beacon Hill, close to his owner's home in Seattle.[11]

At first glance, it might seem possible that memorializing and interring dogs is a relatively new, western European and American phenomenon, merely a remnant of the Victorian cult of domesticity with its idealizing and humanizing of dogs. A seemingly obvious conclusion would be that when this idealization of faithful canines combined with a culture of sanitizing, memorializing, hiding, and denying death, dog cemeteries emerged.[12] To a certain extent current practices of commemorating the canine dead do continue to reflect this particular Victorian sentiment and practice. But there is a kink in this theory because the roots are much deeper than the nineteenth century and they reveal amazing links between humans, dogs, and death that extend into the initial encounters between these two species.

Digging into the First Canine Burials

Is it ritual or rubbish?[13]

At the entrance of a 12,000-year-old dwelling at Ein Mallaha, an ancient site in the upper Jordan Valley, a human skeleton lies close to a large slab of limestone (thus indicating a ritual burial). The skeleton was curled on its right side (damage to the pelvis prevents sex determination, but the individual was old when she or he died). Under the skull, as if to provide a pillow, was the person's left arm. The left hand, in turn, stretched out from under the person's head to rest gently on the chest of a puppy, buried with this older person. Very significantly, the skeleton of the puppy was complete, not a skull alone or a collection of bones alone. This indicates that the puppy was viewed as an intact individual, who needed to

remain such in death as well as life, rather than a symbol or
tool. Based on the teeth and bones, the puppy was probably
four to five months old at the time of death. It is a tender
scene that suggests an affectionate relationship rather than
a purely pragmatic one. The puppy was there because the
deceased human was assumed to desire its presence in the
afterlife for companionship.[14] In other words, the pup was
not a way of providing food in the afterlife, but rather was a
companion in the journey.

There are other examples of remains of animals buried
with humans in this ancient culture, a context that needs to
be considered when pondering why this puppy was placed in
the grave alongside the elderly human companion. A young
man was buried with antlers on his head, possibly to equate
him with hunting and antelopes or other deer-like animals.
Another person was buried with a belt made from animal
teeth. But the relational aspect of the puppy seems to be
unique even amidst these myriad animal-associated grave
goods. The dog was a complete skeleton—a full animal—
buried as a whole in relationship to a whole human being. In
other words, there was not just an item symbolizing the dog,
but the actual dog as a whole creature.

Burials such as this one offer evidence that, from the
earliest days of this interspecies connection, there was something more than solely a utilitarian or symbolic relationship.
Rather, the shared evolution of humans and dog was and
is as deeply ritualistic, religious, and sacred as it was and is
pragmatic. This conclusion comes after considering myriad
examples of intentionally and thoughtfully buried dogs all
over the globe.[15]

Much of the earliest archaeological evidence for dogs is
connected with burial sites deliberately planned by humans.
Over 14,000 years ago, the Bonn-Oberkassel dog was not

only intentionally buried but was interred with humans.[16] Prehistoric dog burials have been discovered on every continent (except Antarctica, where there were no wolves or humans). Following the Bonn-Oberkassel dog, the oldest dogs found thus far are in Siberia and date to over 10,000 years before the present.[17]

In the meantime, there is ample support for the claim that humans extended their relationship with dogs beyond the practical roles in hunting or guarding in this life and into whatever the next life might hold. This expanded role crossed cultural borders; it was widespread, and seems to have, at times at least, crossed hierarchical boundaries as well. Ritual recognition of dogs related to death was not just a frivolous practice of the privileged humans. In far northern Europe (Denmark and Sweden), for example, dogs were buried in the graves of people from different socio-economic classes, and dogs figured centrally in a variety of funerary rituals. In even these very cold climates, dogs were deliberately buried, crouched in a sleeping position and covered with red ochre. It appears that they were also interred with grave goods to carry them through into the afterlife.[18]

While almost all of these early burials are obviously anonymous, as are the human burials, the name and life story of at least one ancient dog is well known because of the incredible attention paid to him after his death. In a burial ground dating from about 2,700–2,600 BCE and located not far from the famous Pyramid of Cheops in Egypt, an inscribed piece of limestone reads,

> The dog which was the guard of His Majesty. Abuwtiyuw was his name. His Majesty ordered that he be buried ceremonially, that he be given a coffin from the royal treasury, fine linen in great quantity, and incense. His Majesty also gave perfumed ointment, and ordered that a tomb be built

for him by the gangs of masons. His Majesty did this for him in order that he (the dog) might be honored before the great god, Anubis.[19]

The archaeologists who discovered this fascinating inscription suggest that the dog likely belonged to a servant of the ruler, but became attached to "His Majesty," barking in order to protect him. Because of this fine canine service in life, the ruler decided to have the dog ritually buried in order to make sure that he would continue such devotion to him in the afterlife as well. No small expense went into the burial, indicating how important it was to the king to have this dog with him for eternity.[20]

The practice of dog burials occurred frequently in Iron Age Britain as well, a time period that extends from about 800 BCE until the Roman conquest of Britain in 43 CE. Archaeological records note numerous "special animal deposits," including one where the body of the dog was covered in large glacial pebbles.[21] This same treatment was given to a number of human skeletons as well, suggesting that at least this particular dog was significant enough to warrant special attention in death.[22] At another site a very small adult dog, a toy-sized breed, was carefully buried late in the period. This rare find—there is little evidence for toy dogs in Britain before the Roman conquest—indicates that there might have been some early trading for very specific types of dogs occurring at that point. Maybe this small dog was a luxury item, a pampered pet for a powerful person whose love continued after death.[23] At other sites large numbers of dog remains were uncovered, for example over fifty dog skulls were found in pits during excavations at Silchester.[24]

The Mediterranean world continues to yield amazing archaeological discoveries related to intentional dog burials. Arguably one of the most significant, and definitely one of the most extensive, is the ancient canine cemetery at Ashkelon (in modern-day Israel) where well over 1,000 dogs were buried during the fifth century BCE.[25] Scholars will never know exactly how many dogs were interred at Ashkelon since a portion of this burial ground is now under the sea, but the evidence is striking. Already over eight hundred dog graves have been excavated, with many more yet to be uncovered. The canines—some very young, even fetal, others adults— are carefully laid to rest on their side with their tail curled between their legs. There was obviously great care given to these burials and, quite likely, some sacred connection here. As the head zoologists of the dig point out, each burial was a "discrete event" since "no skewed heads, or other skeletal distortions that characterize animals that were just pitched into a convenient hole" appear.[26] While the dogs could have played a sacred role, it is important to note that there is no evidence of sacrifice and the age range of the dogs represents a standard mortality spread from mature adults to puppies never having survived into adulthood. In other words, the dogs died of natural causes but were still held in such esteem as to be carefully buried. The lead excavator of the site, Lawrence Stager, suggests that the dogs served as part of a healing cult, maybe even related to the Mesopotamian goddess of healing herself, Gula.[27] It is also interesting to note that the dogs buried at Ashkelon were typical Middle Eastern dogs for that time period. In other words, they were Mediterranean mutts. These dogs were not bred as smaller pets or as aids in hunting or herding, rather they were typical village dogs ritually interred.

During the period when this marvelous dog cemetery was founded at Ashkelon, the people living there were influenced by and in contact with Phoenician culture. Interestingly, archaeologists discovered several dog cemeteries dating to the same period (roughly the 5th century BCE) in other Phoenician influenced cities, though none nearly as impressive as Ashkelon. For example, at nearby Ashdod (also on the coast), archaeologists discovered seven carefully buried dogs. Individual dogs were interred at two other eastern Mediterranean coastal cities—Berytus (modern-day Beirut) and Tel Dor—as well.[28]

By the time Hellenistic culture dominated the Mediterranean world (after Alexander the Great, d. 323 BCE), dogs figured centrally in myriad rituals and mythological systems related to death and the afterlife. Alexander himself had a beloved dog named Peritas whom, according to a report by the historian Plutarch, the conqueror raised from a pup. When Peritas, his dear companion and compatriot, died, the powerful Alexander had him buried with the same ceremonial recognition as a human hero. After his burial, Alexander named the city where Peritas rested for eternity after his deceased dog.[29]

It is not surprising that Greeks held individual dogs in high esteem. In Homer's epic *Odyssey*, the great dog Argus plays a seemingly small, yet very profound, role. Odysseus is returning home after twenty years, but he is disguised as a beggar in order to sneak into his house. As he approaches, Odysseus recognizes his dog Argus, whom he had raised and made into a powerful hunter. At this point Argus has been neglected and is extremely old; he is curled up on a pile of dung. In order to maintain his disguise, Odysseus simply states, "what a noble hound that is." Argus, however, does recognize his master, even after twenty years. While he does not have the strength to stand up, he wags his tail and droops his ears in acknowledgment. Sadly Odysseus cannot respond, except for shedding a single tear and walking by Argus. Knowing that his master has returned, Argus dies. It is this model of canine fidelity and strength that is occasionally remembered and noted in dog burials in the Greek world.

While many of the examples of such burials are touching, one instance offers a particularly poignant window into the sacred role of dogs and death. Inside a well in the Greek town of Eretria, at least twenty-six dogs were buried with at least nineteen human infants. The dogs range in age from neonatal to adult, but the infants were all newborns. While the cause of death of the infants cannot be determined, the presence of specific coins dates this mass burial to the war of Chremonides (267–261 BCE).[30] Maybe the infants, along with their dogs, were slaughtered by the enemy, or a contagious disease rapidly moved through Eretria causing the death of a number of newborns at once. Based on many of the mythologies of the time, which are elaborated more fully below, burying the dogs with these vulnerable children might have been a way to protect them as they journeyed into the afterlife.

With this eternal journey in mind, ancient Greek dog owners spoiled them and recalled them with fondness even in the afterlife. An interesting example was found behind the Stoa of Attalos, the main public building of the ancient Athenian market. Here, a fourth-century grave contained the skeleton of a dog with a large beef bone near his head, possibly food or a toy to sustain him in the underworld.[31] At another location, these moving words were placed on a memorial stone for a deceased dog:

> Thou who passest on the path, if haply thou dost mark this monument,
> Laugh not, I pray thee,
> Though it is a dog's grave; tears fell for me,
> And the dust was heaped above me by a master's hands,
> Who likewise engraved these words upon my tomb.[32]

It seems that Odysseus and Argus were not the only faithful dog-master pair in Greece.[33]

As the Greek period morphs into the Roman era in the Mediterranean world, dog burials remained part of the cultural heritage. Along the north wall of a Roman-era cemetery at Yasmina, in the city of Carthage in Tunisia, another quite

moving human-dog burial was discovered. Here excavations uncovered the third-century CE burial of an adolescent/
young-adult female in a carefully made grave topped with
cobbles and tiles, and with the skeleton of an elderly dog at
the girl's feet. The dog was also buried with one of the few
grave goods found in the cemetery, a glass bowl carefully
placed behind its shoulder. The Yasmina dog, which probably resembled a modern Pomeranian, is an example of a
toy breed. What is more remarkable about the dog is that,
despite a host of physical problems including tooth loss that
likely required him to eat soft foods, osteoarthritis, a dislo-
cated hip, and spinal deformation that would have limited
mobility, the dog had survived into his mid- to late teens. He
was clearly well cared for, and even death could not separate
the dog from his owner. Studying the remains of dog burials,
even those from thousands of years ago, often has an emotional impact on researchers. "Perhaps of all the archaeological cases for pets I can think of," says Michael MacKinnon,
an archaeologist from the University of Winnipeg, "I believe
the Yasmina 'sick' dog is the most poignant."[34]

Ritual burials of dogs continued throughout Europe into
the first century CE. In Sweden burial sites even contain multiple dogs in some of the more elaborate graves. One such
grave, that of a warrior who died sometime in the seventh
century CE, included four dogs of different types. One was
an average height, two were tall and slender, and a final one
was big and stocky. These dogs likely served different purposes in life; for example, the tall, slender ones seem to be
sight hounds for hunting and the large stocky dog may have
been a guard. Regardless, they were significant enough in
the status of the warrior to be incorporated into his funerary
ritual and burial.[35]

But ancient dog burials are not limited to the Mediterranean world and northern Europe. The second-oldest dog

remains excavated from a cave site in Japan, dating from the Jomon period between 8,500 and 8,000 years ago, appear to have been intentionally buried.[36] At this location there were twenty-two dogs, the size of a modern shiba inu, interred. Carefully curled on their sides when they were buried, in a relaxed sleep-like position, they were gently arranged in death to mimic a comfortable position in life. These ancient dogs are likely the ancestors of the seven breeds of dogs eventually recorded as indigenous to Japan.[37]

On the mainland of Asia, almost concurrently with the Jomon burials—so between 9,000 and 7,800 years ago—the oldest Chinese dog burials were also taking place. Eleven dogs were buried at Jiahu in southwestern China. A little over 1,000 years later, dog remains were found with human burials in China as well.[38]

The practice also continued as humans migrated from the African-Eurasian contiguous landmass to new continents. In North America at the Koster site in Illinois, three domestic dog burials date to 8,500 years before the present, as early as the burials in East Asia. This means that the practice occurred relatively soon after the arrival of humans on the North American continent. One particularly rich region for dog burials is the southern tier of what is now the United States, with examples from Tennessee, Kentucky, Alabama, Georgia, Florida, and Mississippi, some almost as old as those at the Koster site, dating back over 8,000 years.

By 6,600 years ago, dog burials were not just widespread in North America but were also associated with human remains. These very early human-dog connected burials occurred on the northwest coast.[39] Here the tradition seems to continue, as people who lived in the area around the Puget Sound (Coast Salish people) buried dogs "ceremonially like humans."[40]

While the burials date significantly later, the practice of burying dogs continued in South America. In Peru, a number of naturally mummified dogs have been recovered, including one dating back 3,000 years. But the vast majority of dog burials thus far discovered there took place about 1,000 years ago. In 2006 archaeologists working in an ancient cemetery near the city of Ilo in southern Peru found the well-preserved remains of eighty dogs interspersed with the burials of about 2,000 people. At that point, the Chiribaya people in Peru valued their dogs enough to make sure they had snacks after death (so they placed fish bones next to their noses), and to make sure they stayed warm (so they were wrapped in carefully woven llama-wool blankets). Some of the dogs are curled on their side with their heads resting gently on pillows.[41]

For most of the 15,000 years that humans and dogs have lived together, they have also died together and sought the afterlife in each other's company. Granted, this was likely not a choice made by the dogs and in some, perhaps most, instances, it was not a timely death for the canines who were forced to accompany humans to the grave. But over these millennia, as humans grappled with the meaning of death, and life, many of them found that dogs contributed in important ways to an understanding, not only of this world, but of whatever world happened after death. The careful, ritual burial of these dogs provided a window into the quest for meaning in the afterlife. And this was not the end of the story.

Dogs at Death's Door and Beyond

Symbolically, the dog is the animal pivot of the human universe, lurking at the threshold.[42]

Argus, the loyal hound who waits two decades for Odysseus to return, is not the only dog in Homer's ancient epics the *Iliad* and the *Odyssey* (8th century BCE). These stories also introduce the hound of Hades (the grisly death god) who guards the gates of the underworld. Herakles (Hercules) has to confront and tame the hound as the last of his labors. Eventually the hound morphs into the three-headed (or fifty-headed) strange beast named Kerberus (Cerberus), still very much a large and intimidating guard dog. Kerberus famously positions the dog in that space between life and death, a role filled by many dogs before and after.

As already noted, one of the most significant aspects of dogs related to human cultural ideas is that they exist somewhere in the betwixt and between, in the threshold. Not fully animal, but not fully human, they both bridge the gap and exist within it. They connect humans to nature while simultaneously providing a border between humans and nature. When they are included in the mythologies surrounding death, the idea is extended and humans have frequently considered dogs those who hover in the doorway between life and death, just as they hover between nature and culture, human and animal.[43] Representations of this phenomenon in mythologies and practices surrounding death and dying are found far beyond the well-known image of Kerberus. Just as he guarded the Underworld in Hellenistic culture, two dogs appear guarding the similar mythological and symbolic gates across Eurasia.[44]

This belief is reflected in a variety of interesting practices. One of these is the ritual of burying dogs to the west of houses. During the Bronze Age, evidence of dog burials in west-facing doorways appears from England to China. There are likely a variety of reasons for this practice. First, archaeologists speculate that dogs were buried by the doorways to protect the household from unwanted intruders among the dead. In other words, living dogs guarded the house from living intruders and dead dogs guarded the house from trespassers from the underworld. Just as Kerberus guards the Underworld, keeping the living out and the dead in, so the buried, and possibly sacrificed, dog guards against otherworldly forces that might try to invade the home. This transition—guardian of gateways both in life and in death—continues to reinforce the liminality of the dog.

Second, not just in the Hellenistic world, but throughout Indo-European and Indo-Iranian cultural areas, different mythologies consider dogs as guardians of the gate to the Otherworld, which was often placed to the west with the setting sun, thus reinforcing the practice.[45] In the *Rig Veda*, an ancient Indic text, Yama, the lord of the dead, is accompanied by two dogs. The dead are instructed to "run on the right path, past the brindled, four-eyed dogs" to get to the ancestors. Here, the dogs are described as "dark messengers of Yama with flaring nostrils" who threaten the dead. But in the same hymn "the four-eyed keepers of the path" are also entrusted to "watch over" the deceased on their journey.[46] So dogs are "both-and," complicated figures who both threaten and protect. Another closely related text, the Zoroastrian-Iranian *Avesta*, describes dogs connected to the god Yama. In the Zoroastrian context, however, dogs hold a somewhat less ambiguous role. Known as the "second good creatures after the human beings," dogs "charm [death] away" from the corpse "with their sight," basically protecting the human from the defilement that accompanies death.[47] Dogs are seen as so powerful in Zoroastrian practices related to death that they are even allowed to fill the role of one of the two necessary attendants in funeral rites. The dogs are the "second good creatures" who can accompany the human into death.[48] So burying dogs as guardians of the threshold in this life and the next, and from dangers both in this world and the spirit world, was a fitting practice.

Sacrificing dogs, particularly puppies, to serve as messengers or companions after death also seems to have been a common practice throughout much of the ancient Mediterranean world. Homer's writing offers yet another insight about this practice. In the *Iliad* Achilles is tasked with performing funeral rites for his friend Patroklos. Various customary sacrifices were made—sheep and cows whose fats were used for wrapping the body before placing it on the funeral pyre. But Achilles added something to this. He had four horses, twelve Trojan youths, and two of Patroklos' nine dogs ("dogs fed from the table") offered on the funeral pyre as well.[49] It is hard to know the precise motivation for these sacrifices without additional information, but the sacrificed dogs were most likely either viewed as companions in the Underworld or were simply pets who were killed in order to stay with their master. Regardless of the motivation for sacrificing them, these two dogs had been fed directly from Patroklos' table, so the perceived need to maintain their presence at his death and into the afterlife is stirring.

Along with Kerberus, one of the most readily recognizable canine religious figures is Anubis, the dog-headed god of the Egyptians. His role was to protect the necropolis, the city of the dead, and to oversee the appropriate process of mummification. Ancient Egyptians believed that Anubis actually invented embalming, so he is frequently portrayed in imagery in this role of cemetery god. For example, at one location that dates from almost 2,000 years BCE—the tomb of a pharaoh of Egypt, Senwosret III—there are not only images of Anubis, but the tomb is actually constructed beneath a pyramid-shaped sacred mount named the "Mountain-of-Anubis."[50] In other words, it had a double-Anubis effect.

While this god was a kind of "super-canid" (dog, jackal, fox), the recent rediscovery of a dog catacomb underneath a temple of Anubis is shedding new light on the role of dogs in this Egyptian cult of the dead.[51] Located close to the ancient capital of Memphis, this area was likely the burial ground for the city. This labyrinthine catacomb provides the most stunning example yet of ritual dog burial. There are over eight million dogs mummified and buried here. In this massive catacomb, some individual dogs are buried in niches along the corridors. Some of these dogs would have been offerings to the god, but others may well have lived in the temple grounds as representatives of Anubis. Since the catacomb dates to late in the Egyptian dynastic period (747–730 BCE) it could indicate the ascendancy of dogs in the canid-association of Anubis. In other words, the god was becoming more definitely dog related and less jackal or fox connected. This must represent a period when the role of the dog as messenger between the worlds of the living and the dead was also very important, and these dogs would have been used as intermediaries for those who interred them here. On what could be considered a tragic, even horrible, note, it is highly likely that the equivalent of modern-day puppy mills were located nearby to provide dogs for whatever ritual practices, ending in mummification, were highlighted here. The dogs were killed over a relatively short period, just a couple of decades. While these were not strictly sacrifices, because offering the dogs was seen "as a pious act, with the animal acting as intermediary between the donor and the gods," the scale of the catacombs is striking.[52]

Anubis was not the only deity who seemed to require the sacrifice of puppies. Hekate, sometimes called the "divine friend of dogs" or "Skylakagetis," which means "leader of dogs," was a protective goddess who could ward off evil.[53] Her approach was heralded by her hounds, and one way to make an offering to her was to leave meat at crossroads (which was then likely eaten by pariah dogs). At least four locations of her temples, including Athens, practiced dog sacrifice, and a shrine to her on one of the Greek islands is described as "the cave of the goddess to whom dogs are slain."[54]

Over the course of 1,000 years (approximately 600 BCE– 400 CE), various Celtic people developed complex cultures throughout most of Europe north of the Alps. Their beliefs and practices included dogs—not only as workers in the all-important hunt (as mentioned in chapter 1), but as companions in the afterlife. Particularly fascinating are the chthonic connections, links to the underworld symbolized frequently, in the case of some Celtic tribes, through water. Like those in Egypt, these dogs were often sacrificed, by contrast with those found at sites such as Ashkelon who seem to have died from natural causes before being ritually interred. Dogs at these Celtic sites were often buried in deep wells and pits, or close to other ritual sites. At an ancient site in Danebury, located in southern England, archaeologists discovered the bones of two dogs carefully buried over 2,500 years ago. The dogs were covered with chalk blocks over which the people built a huge timber structure.[55]

In addition to the physical remains of dogs ritually buried by humans, the dog as a figurative bridge between life and death was represented in art throughout the ancient Mediterranean world for thousands of years. Sarcophagi of the wealthy frequently included dog companions carved into the marble or stone (figure 4). These dogs lovingly gaze at the humans, also carved into the stone for eternity, and remind those still living that canines are a monument to both fidelity and adoration.

Other human-dog burial themes continue through the years in European funerary art. Just as the dog in Roman times was buried at the feet of the young woman in Carthage, cathedrals all over Europe during the Middle Ages and the Renaissance have dogs placed at the feet of the dead. This

Figure 4
This small bulldog gazes up at his mistress, Ilaria del Carretto,
from the foot of her sarcophagus (sculpted by Jacopo della
Quercia, c. 1406). The sarcophagus is housed in the Cathedral of
Lucca, Italy. Photo by the author.

symbolism is widespread, with examples in Italy, France, Great Britain, and more. The faithful dog companion continues to accompany humans into the afterlife in these amazing sculptures. As stated so clearly by David White, and as displayed so beautifully in countless pieces of art, "it is not so much that the dog's role extends beyond the world of the living into that of the dead, but rather that the dog's place lies between one world and another."[56]

Maybe it is this romanticized, and frequently actualized, fidelity of dogs that also added to their role as constant mourners. Reports of dogs who attend to a person's grave, or continue to wait for someone to return, are myriad. The death of the young artist Charles Gough offers one account of such canine devotion.[57] In April 1805 Gough left on a hiking trip in the English Lake District, accompanied only by his dog. Three months later, following the sounds of a dog barking, a local shepherd found Gough's body guarded still by his faithful pup. Gough appeared to have fallen and died from head injuries, his body perched close to the edge of a cliff.[58] The devoted dog became something of a legend, depicted in paintings and even praised in a poem written by William Wordsworth—"Fidelity":

> Yes, proof was plain that since the day
> On which the Traveller thus had died
> The Dog had watch'd about the spot,
> Or by his Master's side:
> How nourish'd here through such long time
> He knows, who gave that love sublime,
> And gave that strength of feeling, great
> Above all human estimate.[59]

Various other accounts of supreme canine fidelity in the face of the death of a beloved are reported across cultures. One of the most well known is the story of Hachiko, an akita inu who lived in the early twentieth century in Japan. As a puppy, Hachiko was taken in by Professor Ueno, a teacher at a local college. Each day, the dog would go to the train station at just the right time to meet his owner. But one day, Ueno did not get off the train. He had suffered a cerebral hemorrhage and died at work. Still, for years, Hachiko continued the routine, waiting for his owner's return.[60] Eventually the akita became quite famous and there was even a statue erected in his honor at the train station.[61] Frequent, similar accounts are reported worldwide, thus reinforcing the long-standing connections between dogs, death, mourning, and faithfulness.

Mourning the Beloved Dog

"Just this side of heaven there is a place called the Rainbow Bridge."[62]

While the modern practice of memorializing dogs might have been reframed by the sentiments of the Victorian era, it did not stop there. As of 2009, according to the International Association of Pet Cemeteries and Crematories, there were over six hundred pet cemeteries in the United States. Primarily an urban phenomenon in their modern incarnation, and certainly marked by changing burial practices for humans as well (primarily the professionalizing of mortuary practice and removal of it from the sphere of the home), thousands of dogs are interred and cremated each year at these modern pet burial grounds.

And this phenomenon is emerging in other parts of the world as well. For example, fascinating research on pet burials in contemporary Japan provides a series of illustrations of shifting funerary practices that frequently include dogs.[63] In post–World War II Japan, as the economy rebounded, pet-keeping became a marker of entry into the middle-class. With that cultural shift, lapdogs (chin) became increasingly popular. By the early twenty-first century, dogs were viewed as family members by over 70 percent of their owners in Japan.[64] Following such a major change in how dogs fit into the culture, including as part of the familial system of memorialization and responsibility, the number of pet cemeteries in Japan exploded and there are now an estimated 600–900. Considering the fact that Japan is an island nation with increasing competition for land, this is quite an impressive commitment of resources. Traditional Buddhist burial rites are even invoked, and pet spirits are being reframed as "benevolent companions" rather than vengeful spirits.[65]

Arguably, though, the most intriguing contemporary memorials to dogs are in the electronic world. A quick Internet search of "The Rainbow Bridge"—a poem shared by many dog lovers to mark the death of their companions—yields thousands of hits. Grief support groups are expanding to fill a gap: the significant impact of the loss of a pet on the human survivors, which is just now being recognized by psychologists and therapists as a serious topic. And on Monday evenings, people throughout the world light candles to remember their pets who have died. These fascinating Internet-global connections between those grieving the loss of their dog companions mark a new stage in the shared journey to the afterlife. Frequently there is an additional layer of grief and guilt associated with the death of these dogs, since humans had often chosen to have their companion humanely euthanized as the dog approached the time of death. Questions are raised about whether or not the person waited too long, or gave up too soon. Veterinarians are frequently called upon to manage these difficult encounters with distraught dog owners.[66]

As many dog owners already know, the impact of the death of a companion dog can be quite significant. In the 2012 Home Box Office documentary, *One Nation Under Dog: Stories of Fear, Loss and Betrayal*, the producers claimed "Americans have always had a love affair with canines."[67] They explore this love affair, in part, by investigating how people deal with the death of a dog. When asked about her recently deceased dog, one woman interviewed expressed the depth of her grief in this way:

> I lost my dog Shaman. He taught me to sit . . . I mean, I taught him to sit, but he taught me to sit too . . . with his nose in the air and eyes half-closed . . . just taking in everything. I'd just smile because everything made sense.

He wasn't my child, he wasn't my parent, he wasn't my partner, he was my dog, and that's much more than you know. We just don't have words for that.[68]

Obviously, Shaman's death had a major emotional impact on his person—it held deep meaning, and his loss as a companion and a friend was beyond her ability to put into words.

For thousands of years, humans have imagined death, in part at least, through the lens of dogs and their cohabitation. Taking no chances at being alone, humans have considered dogs likely and worthy companions. Certainly this phenomenon is growing in the twenty-first century, but mounting evidence points to the fact that dogs have accompanied humans into the afterlife for thousands of years. Victorian and modern-day pet owners who bury their dogs in cemeteries are not part of a small group with extreme relationships to those canines. Rather they seem to hold a pronounced version of widely held beliefs and attitudes, which overall serve to diminish, if not entirely obliterate, the categorical distinction between animal and human.[69]

Chapter 3

- - - - - - - - -

Healing and Saving
Life Is Better with Dogs

*When my younger son, Owen, and I were both seriously
ill—him with liver failure, me with an aggressive prostate
cancer—Bijou became even more than verb and miracle.
She was a healing presence in our lives. Believe me, when
your life is reduced to a huge question mark, nothing feels
better than having a twenty-three-pound mutt snuggled
up next to you. Owen and I both profoundly understood
what a difference a dog makes.[1]*

The "Dogs Detect Cancer Project" is making incredible
discoveries. Working with dog trainers and cancer researchers, the project is tapping into the amazing sense of smell,
along with the eagerness to work, demonstrated by some
highly motivated dogs. The goal is to save lives by detecting
cancer early, earlier than is possible using any other available tests.[2] Researchers capture breath samples for the dogs
to smell, and the dogs are trained to alert when they detect
cancer cells in a sample. This is the same process employed to
train dogs to find drugs, identify arson, or search for missing
people by detecting odor. Amazingly, or maybe not so amazingly for those who understand how sensitive and accurate a

dog's sense of smell is, there is a 98 percent accuracy rate in the tests conducted for lung and breast cancer.[3] Another benefit to this process is that the procedure is non-invasive. But most significantly, the possibilities for very early detection go beyond any traditional medical tests available. Dogs display the ability to alert to "in situ, or stage zero, cancer." Whereas humans, according to medical doctors, can often smell cancer on the breath when it has developed to stage 3 or 4 (late term cancer), tests suggest that dogs can smell cancer when it is still in the very beginning stages of development—earlier than any other cancer screening available, even the most advanced technological approaches.

This detection ability is based on something that has served dogs, and humans, well and helped them survive together for millennia—that incredible canine sense of smell. Dogs can smell at a sensitivity level that is almost beyond human comprehension. It is 10,000 to 100,000 times as acute as the human sense of smell.[4] As one researcher noted, a dog can smell one rotten apple in a barrel of two million.[5] From the moment they are born, dogs rely on their noses. Watching puppies right when they enter the world is amazing. After the mom cleans the pups and gets the newborns breathing, they immediately sniff their way to her. The puppies have no vision or hearing yet, and as a matter of fact their eyes and ears might not open until they are two weeks old. So they rely on their ability to smell their way to their mother to nurse.[6] Observing tiny puppies navigate the world with their noses is revealing. Indeed, it seems to be the primary way they experience their world.

However, the ability to smell certain proteins or chemicals in human bodies is not the only way that dogs are moving into the modern world of medicine. Scientific research points to myriad ways dogs can assist in the healing process, some very straightforward and technical, others based on their emotional impact on humans (which then leads to physiological changes). As already mentioned, their acute sense of smell is tapped in order to indicate cancer, but their powerful nose is also used to alert for seizures in people with epilepsy or signal the onset of hypoglycemia in diabetics. But the list does not stop there. Tests indicate that dogs' ability to provide companionship lowers blood pressure and heart rates.[7] Their work as service animals opens up connections for humans who are sometimes abandoned, ignored, or ostracized. And, in cultures increasingly concerned about obesity epidemics, dogs keep people active and moving. Thinking about and using dogs as healers in scientific and in intuitive ways is not a new phenomenon, even though some of the testing and methodologies have changed. Not surprisingly, dogs have been healing humans for thousands of years and in some amazing ways, even before advanced scientific methods could prove the benefits. From their presence at healing temples in the ancient Mesopotamian world to their work as therapy dogs bringing peace and calm to sites of tragedy, dogs can cure what ails humans.

Soothing Saliva, Purifying Pups

"Lingua canis dum lingit vulnus curat."
(Latin, "A dog's tongue, licking a wound, heals it.")[8]

There was a rich man who was dressed in purple and fine linen and who feasted sumptuously every day. And at his gate lay a poor man named Lazarus, covered with sores, who longed to satisfy his hunger with what fell from the rich man's table; even the dogs would come and lick his sores.

—*Luke 16:19-21 (NRSV)*[9]

Images and statues of Saint Lazarus the Leper almost always include two dogs who are gently licking his sores (figure 5).

Figure 5
Detail from "Madonna and Child with Saints Lazarus Bishop
and Lazarus Leper" (Pietro Francesco Sacchi, 1518–1520,
held in the Cathedral Museum, Genoa, Italy). Photo by the
author.

Usually the saint is propped on crutches and dressed in rags, symbolic of his position as the poor beggar whose only companions were the devoted dogs. His statues are paraded at Good Friday processions to recall his story, which was told by Jesus and recounted in the gospels. While the rich man ignored Lazarus completely, the canines remained his faithful companions. It is a common picture in myth and legend, dogs attending to ailing humans and working to heal their wounds. The connection emerged thousands of years ago as the gods and goddesses associated with healing began to share sacred space with dogs. And at curative shrines from Rome to Babylon to the British Isles, dogs were central players.

One of the earliest clues comes from the ancient Mesopotamian world where the powerful Sumerian-Babylonian goddess Gula, consort of the storm god, was revered as the great healer.[10] Veneration of this goddess of healing endured for well over 1,000 years, likely longer as she morphed into different forms of the same goddess in surrounding cultures. Prayers, dedications, and incantations for recovery from illness or injury were sent to her. Interestingly, some of these prayers survive as carvings on small dog statues offered to the goddess. Not only through the prayer offerings carved into these clay canine figurines, but also in her sacred iconography, Gula is frequently accompanied by a dog. Sometimes she is pictured sitting on a throne which rests on a dog, and at other times the goddess is flanked by her dog and stars.[11] The stars are important because in Babylonian astrology, Gula's constellation is comprised of stars that form the shape of the goddess and her dog gazing at each other.[12] Also known as "Lady of Health," her main cultic center, at Isin, was called the "Dog Temple of Ninisina."[13] The temple at Isin was identified as a Gula-related healing site primarily because of the presence of dogs in the remains. These were not only clay figurines of dogs, though those also provided a hint, but there were also ritual burials of real dogs at this temple. These dog burials date back to 1,000 BCE.[14]

But Gula is not just represented as a female human accompanied by a dog—she becomes a dog herself. By the seventh to fifth centuries BCE, this canine incarnation was the primary way to portray the "Lady of Health." In some of these amazing images, a dog (now symbolizing Gula) is sitting on an elevated platform with a worshiper facing her; the person's hands are raised in a typical pose denoting veneration.[15] The incredibly close identification of dogs and the goddess helps to explain this ancient Assyrian list of activities that were offenses against Gula:

> He did what did not please Gula but turned his face (away)
> so as not to know (it): He saw an injured dog and turned

his face (away). Dogs fought and howled; he saw, but turned his face (away) so as not to know. He saw a dead dog but did not bury (it).[16]

As late as the rule of King Nebuchadnezzar II (604–562 BCE), gold, silver, and bronze dogs were offered at Gula's temple in Babylon in the hopes of curing illness.[17] While it is unclear whether these temples served as the hospitals of their time, the link between Gula, dogs, and healing is unmistakable.

Dogs also became apotropaic forces, powerful balances in opposing malevolence or guarding against the "evil eye." While this might seem a strange way to conceive of dogs as "healers," in many cultures illness was (and still is) equated with possession by evil or demonic forces. In some of these contexts, ancient Babylonia and Assyria to name just two, the rabid dog was seen as particularly powerful. Because of this rulers often placed images of the rabid dog at the gates of their palaces and temples to ward off evil and, by association, disease.[18] In this context dogs are, once again, an in-between, ambiguous animal. As polluted (rabid), they also purify.

Fascinating healing rituals involving puppies were also part of Hittite culture, which thrived in Anatolia from approximately 1800 to 1100 BCE. In their "Ritual of Zuwi" the Hittites would hold a puppy up to a patient and say, "I hold it (the puppy) to him with the right hand saying 'just as the puppy licks its own nine body parts'—and I call the person by name—'in the same way let it lick up the illness in this one's body parts.'"[19] But, just as some other forms of ritual healing and purification involving dogs and other animals did not end well for the animal, the dogs and puppies frequently ended up as sacrifices in these ceremonies. Puppies, in particular, were understood to take on the illness, often believed to be an incarnation of evil, from the patient and would then be killed in order to get rid of the wickedness. As noted elsewhere, dogs were not always happy survivors at the temples:

they were frequently sacrifices and forced emissaries to the underworld.

As is the case in the images of St. Lazarus, dogs are commonly pictured licking wounds. History reveals this long-standing tradition of trusting the saliva of dogs as a healing agent—and a powerful one at that. But there is mounting evidence that moves dogs beyond this symbolic role of caretaker. Recently scientists have in fact discovered healing properties in dog saliva. It contains antibacterial and, possibly, other properties that cause wounds to heal more quickly.[20] While still a debated idea, and one that needs to be balanced with the possibility that there are also properties in dog saliva that could cause infection, it is an intriguing prospect and one that was obviously considered by people thousands of years ago as they opened their healing temples to the dogs. As ancient Armenian legends claimed, the dogs "lick the wounds of injured men and revive them."[21]

This association with dogs and healing is also present in the iconography, veneration, and practice connected to a Greek god that many people might still find familiar: Asklepios. While frequently portrayed with a snake, Asklepios—the longest enduring of the ancient gods of medicine and one who is still invoked by physicians (at least symbolically) into the modern period—was also closely associated with dogs.[22] As his legend goes, Asklepios, the son of the god Apollo and a mortal woman, was yanked from his mother's womb and then abandoned to the elements by his father. But Asklepios was saved, maybe by the intervention of the goddess of nature, through the tender care of a female sheepdog. The sheepdog nursed and protected the abandoned infant-god. Interestingly, in the legends from this particular area, Epidauros in Greece, which was the center of Asklepios' cult, there is a mountain sanctuary located on Mount Kynortion, the "Mountain of the Rising Dog." With this sacred location and story as background, from that point forward, dogs were associated with Asklepios' imagery and his temples.[23]

Temples to Asklepios are found throughout the Hellenistic world, and some of the healings at these temples are attributed directly to dogs: "A child was cured of a growth on his neck by the tongue of a dog. A blind boy received his sight the same way."[24] Not all instances of dogs assisting in healing at Asklepios' temples were as benign, however. They would also play a role in diagnosing "strange illnesses." In these cases, "a dog, through contact with an ill person, was thought to contract the disease, and was then killed and examined to determine its nature."[25] Reminiscent of the puppies who took on pollution and evil in the "Ritual of Zuwi," these dogs of Asklepios were believed to absorb, literally, the illness of the human and then become the cure by being sacrificed.

Concepts of purity and pollution intersected in dogs, making their ambivalent role both powerful and vulnerable. Frequently, as was the case in rituals in Greece and Anatolia, to be healed was to be purified. And dogs, often puppies, were the cure, a deadly combination for the young canines. When explaining why a dog was sacrificed, Plutarch lays this out clearly:

> Is it because this performance constitutes a rite of purification for the city? . . . Nearly all the Greeks used a dog as the sacrificial victim for ceremonies of purification; and some, at least, make use of it to this day. They bring forth for Hecate puppies along with other materials for purification, and rub round about with puppies such persons as are in need of cleansing. (*Roman Questions*, 68)[26]

After thousands of years living side by side, ideas of healing, purification, and the underworld were all part of a complex package of symbolism piled onto dogs.

Other ancient pieces of evidence point to the presence of dogs as guardians, as well as healers, at the temples of Asklepios. One such account from the second century CE describes a "temple-thief" who came to Asklepios' shrine in Athens to steal offerings. The thief waited until the guards all fell asleep, but little did he know that there was an "excellent watcher, a Dog," in the temple as well. The dog barked "with all its might" even though the thief pelted it with stones. Apparently the dog then followed the thief home and continued to bark, attracting other Athenians to the scene. When they discovered the loud canine was a temple guardian, they arrested the thief. Following this, the dog was rewarded "by being fed and cared for at the public expense for being a faithful watcher and second to none of the attendants in vigilance."[27]

Some of these ancient gods and goddesses of healing might be connected to each other over time and space, with the dog tagging along for the medicinal ride. An interesting hypothesis suggests that the name "Asklepios" could be linked to the city of Ashkelon where over a thousand dogs were buried in the fifth century BCE.[28] It seems likely that the burials of these myriad dogs at Ashkelon could be related to a healing cult there, a cult that carries on the tradition of the goddess Gula, thus providing a segue from Mesopotamia to Greece.[29]

The practice of keeping dogs as healers spread throughout the Mediterranean world, possibly as part of the proliferation of these cults connected to the descendants of Gula and Asklepios. A fascinating example of this practice is the "Yasmina dog" discussed above, the small arthritic Maltese-type dog buried with an adolescent in a Roman cemetery.[30] This dog was very likely not only a beloved pet, but also a healing companion. In the year 264 BCE, Callimachus, an ancient Greek author, reported that Maltese dogs were laid upon the stomachs of ill individuals to "draw out and ease pain." Thus the practice of carrying the small dog close to the chest grew in popularity. The Yasmina dog, who had very few teeth and was quite arthritic (therefore requiring significant care), was worth that effort because of the healing effects he had on the child with whom he was eventually put to rest.[31]

Asklepios' healing power, and that of his dogs, is evident as far north as the British borders of the Roman Empire. Early in the nineteenth century, ten dog votives—some statues, some plaques—dating from the third to fourth centuries CE were discovered around the remains of the Lydney temple in Gloucestershire, England. One of these, a lovely bronze statuette, appears to be a type of greyhound. The dog looks gently over his shoulder with ears flat against his head. One of the plaques pictures an alert dog with her tail extended and her body in a playful bow position. Below her is a written dedication to Nodens, the god to whom this temple was dedicated. Because of the prevalence of dogs at the site, researchers decided to dig more deeply into Roman-era symbolism of dogs. Eventually, based on the fascinating evidence at Lydney, it became obvious that the temple was a healing shrine with connections to Asklepios. In addition, there are strong indications that fertility rituals, often connected to healing, also occurred at this location—a link that became fairly common in ancient Mediterranean and European traditions.

Roman era religious sites throughout western (primarily Celtic and Saxon) Europe continue with a similar theme—healing, fertility, the underworld and, of course, dogs. As Celtic and Roman traditions merged, the always flexible dog remained central. For example, over a hundred stone altars to Nehalennia, a deity of the North Sea and protector of the people, still exist, even though her temples long ago washed away. These stone altars depict the goddess with a large dog sitting patiently at her feet. Many of these same images also include baskets of fruit and bread, pointing to the connection between fertility, protection, dogs, and healing.

Various other Celtic goddesses were portrayed with small dogs on their laps, possibly hinting at their role in healing. These goddesses appear from Luxembourg to Triers to Canterbury.[32] Some followers of these goddesses would respond in kind. For example, at a sanctuary for Sequana, the goddess of the sources of the Seine River, votive objects depict devotees holding dogs in their hands.[33] In Britain the Triple Mother goddesses, associated not only with healing but, again, with fertility, hold swaddled lapdogs. Sometimes they are nursing these dogs, other times offering them fruit.[34]

The evidence of dogs connected to healing deities and shrines in the ancient Mediterranean and European world is seemingly endless. Both symbolically, as figurines or offerings to the gods, and bodily, as the ones licking wounds and sitting on laps or as the ones sacrificed to purify a suffering human, dogs have been trusted as healers for thousands of years. Just as humans continue to seek how best to address illness, dogs accompany them.

Medieval Saints Tell Tales of Tails

A plaque on the side of the small rural road in southern France identifies the "Bois de St. Guignefort" (Woods of St. Guignefort). Here, it states, according to legend is where the cult of this saint thrived until an official of the Catholic Church, the Dominican heretic-hunter Stephen of Bourbon, tried to destroy the cult in the thirteenth century. But that was neither the beginning nor the end of the story. Saint Guignefort was no ordinary, run-of-the-mill saint—as a matter of fact, he was a dog. As his legend goes, Guignefort had nobly protected the infant in his care by killing a "serpent maximus" (huge snake) who was trying to crawl into the child's crib.

But when the parents heard the baby screaming and ran to the room, they were met with a blood-covered scene and a toppled bassinet. Assuming the worst of the dog the father immediately shot an arrow into Guignefort's heart. Tragically, when they approached the infant the parents found the snake, scooped up their unharmed child, and realized that Guignefort was a hero.

The dog, who was executed "unjustly," was buried on the manor grounds under a "great pile of stones" and in the midst of a grove of trees. Peasants in the area heard about the "noble dog" and venerated him as a martyr. Women, in particular, would bring "sick or weak children" to the resting place of Guignefort, and quickly he became known as a local saint and healer. Guignefort was a child-protecting, gentle, healing greyhound. And though Stephen of Bourbon tried his best, by digging up the dog's bones, burning them, and throwing them into the river, one heretic-hunter could not halt Guignefort's impact. For generations before Stephen arrived, the local people had believed that he would help heal their sick children. And for centuries after Stephen made his declaration claiming that Guignefort was a heretic, the people continued to bring their children to his shrine in the woods, disregarding the order of the Church.

It seems that the saint was a particularly powerful healer for children with mobility problems. Generations of children's shoes are deposited around his shrine. As late as the early 1900s, there is evidence of parents bringing their children to Saint Guignefort, asking for his healing spirit for their afflicted offspring. While veneration of the dog-saint waned over the course of the twentieth century, that decline lasted only a hundred years. In the early twenty-first century, devotees of the saint are again telling his story and reviving his legend.[35]

Other medieval saints, while not dogs themselves, have dogs at their sides when they offer healing in times of turmoil.

Saint Roch of Montpellier was born in the late thirteenth century. According to his hagiographies, Roch lost his parents when he was young and gave away his possessions, determined to make a pilgrimage to Rome. On the way, Roch stopped frequently to care for victims of the plague. Reportedly, he healed many with the sign of the cross. After reaching Rome, it was time for Roch to begin his return journey, but everything did not go as planned. Roch himself came down with the plague after so much exposure. Unwilling to expose others to this deadly disease, he hid himself in the woods. There, a friendly dog brought him bread each day and licked his wounds, literally saving the saint's life. From that point forward, Roch, patron saint of those suffering from the plague, is always pictured with a dog next to him. Images of St. Roch and his dog adorn the churches of Europe from Italy to Belgium to Poland to Spain. Always accompanied by his dog, the saint points to a wound on his leg (a sore from the plague, undoubtedly). And his canine companion, gazing up attentively, offers the saint the piece of bread gently held in his mouth.[36]

In the late sixteenth century, the body of St. Roch was moved to Venice, Italy. It was an appropriate location for a saint and his dog who were believed to be powerful protectors against the plague, since that city, a major center of commerce, was prone to exposure to contagious disease spreading throughout the Mediterranean world. Under orders from the pope, several fabulous churches were built there in Roch's honor, and a confraternity (basically a local church-related social service group) with a hospital attached was established. When plague or pestilence moved through Venice, Roch and his dog were invoked as healers. A particularly horrible round of the plague swept through Venice in 1630–1631. Over a quarter of the population died, dealing a huge blow to the Venetians.[37] But, from all accounts, the people received comfort and hope from the presence of the saint and his dog, and from the confraternity associated with them who, in the tradition of Roch, worked to care for the sick and dying citizens.

"A Helping Hound"[38]

If your dog is fat, you aren't getting enough exercise.[39]

The Mighty Texas Dog Walk topped the *Guinness Book of World Records'* list for the most dogs in a walk at one place at one time for several years.[40] People and their dogs gather for this event in Austin, Texas, every April to raise funds for Texas Hearing and Service Dogs (THSD), an organization that places trained helping dogs with people who need them. This Texas group is one of hundreds in the world that recognize the incredible health and well-being value of human-dog teams, particularly for those humans who have certain physical or mental issues that keep them from participating fully in society. An added benefit is that dogs in the THSD program are all rescued from animal shelters; they are homeless dogs looking for a place in the world. The partnership has proven magical. In the last twenty years, THSD has taken in over 700 homeless dogs from shelters in the state and, after intensive training, placed these dogs with human partners to enrich their lives.

Dogs have spent over ten millennia healing humans in various ways—from licking their wounds to assisting their deities. And in the twenty-first century, the value of this healing capacity is recognized not only by groups like THSD, who train dogs for service, but by the scientific community, too. As early as 1980, public health studies were tracking heart attack survivors and noticed surprising results. Dog owners were 8.6 times more likely to be alive one year after a heart attack than those without dogs.[41] There are myriad reasons why this might be the case, including the fact that dogs do force you to exercise more, laugh longer, and go outside.[42]

Studies pointing to the health benefits of dog ownership conducted over the last thirty years are too numerous to cite—a fact that says something in and of itself. But they point to a consistent list of positive impacts, including but not limited to: stress reduction, decrease of depression, lowering of blood pressure, lowering of triglyceride and cholesterol levels, lower rates of allergies in children.[43] An additional benefit is the decreased cost of health care for pet owners. For example, in nursing homes across New York, Missouri, and Texas, the average cost of medications dropped from $3.80 per patient per day to $1.18 per day when dogs were present.[44]

"Guide dogs for the mind" is a prototype program established by students at the Glasgow School of Art in partnership with Alzheimers Scotland and Dogs for the Disabled.[45] Just as dogs work with people who have vision and hearing disabilities, these guide dogs work with people who have dementia. The dogs are trained to remind people to take their medications (by delivering a chew-proof bag to them at a certain time of day), eat and sleep at appropriate times, and generally maintain routines that will keep them healthier. Dogs are masters of routines, maintaining them adeptly. This is a central concern for humans with dementia. When a dog knows that it is time for dinner, she will be relentless until you feed her. The guide dog will force a person with dementia to go to the dog food—where there will also be a note reminding the person that it's time for their dinner as well. An added benefit is exercise and social interaction; if you have a dog, you are much more likely to get out and walk—and the dog will make sure you make it back home safely.

Numerous organizations worldwide work to train and place service dogs with people who need them. Pet Partners, like THSD, states explicitly that it is committed to the idea that people are "healthier and happier because companion, service and therapy animals enrich and positively impact their everyday lives."[46] They have over 11,000 volunteer teams who work in health care and therapy settings throughout the United States. The benefits are astounding. Not only do service dogs provide basic, pragmatic assistance—opening doors, picking up objects, alerting to sounds such as a doorbell—but they can also open up the social world for people with disabilities. Service dogs, in other words, provide much more than functional assistance. Attachment and caregiving needs are also filled. As one woman, who had been in dysfunctional human relationships for over twenty-two years, stated, her dog "taught her how to bond" with humans again as well.[47]

Autism Assistance Dogs are a relatively new phenomenon, but their impact is being felt widely. Rates of autism are rising significantly in the U.S.—from 1 in 150 in reporting year 2000 to 1 in 88 in reporting year 2008.[48] Autistic children are literally "anchored" to their trained dogs, allowing parents and children to spend more quality time together rather than spending time constantly monitoring each other. The assistance dogs also decrease the common tantrums and "meltdowns" experienced by autistic children by providing them with a distraction or release. Amazingly, in many cases, dogs also bring autistic children out of their shells, as the children learn to attach to another being and to trust without judgment.[49]

Training programs for dogs can also rehabilitate the human trainers. Puppies Behind Bars places young dogs, identified as potential service dogs, with prison inmates for months of training and socialization.[50] The goal is to work with these dogs and build up their confidence, teaching them over eighty commands in the process, thus preparing them to become service dogs in any number of capacities—seeing eye dogs, hearing ear dogs, war veteran support dogs, and more. In the process, inmates at various correctional facilities build up their own confidence, experience the unconditional love and judgment-free relationships that the puppies offer, and learn new skills that they can apply when they finish serving their sentences. It's a win-win situation for all the players—human and dog alike—and it changes countless lives.

While connections with companion dogs are almost always very intense and emotional, arguably those with service dogs are even more so. Certified service dogs are allowed to go everywhere with their human companions, so they frequently spend every waking and sleeping moment in each other's company. For over nine years, Beauty was an assistance dog. When Beauty died, her person described the depth of their connection:

> She was a piece of me. She's not just a dog, she's not just a companion, she's not just there to help you, she's there through all thick and thin of your life . . . When my husband told me "B is gone," I know I cried in such a way I'd never cried before . . . It's like my heart broke in two . . . I think about B and the good things that she did, and that she's not suffering anymore, and that she worked her job really well, and she showed me what love can do.[51]

Televisions around the U.S. and the world projected the horror as news unfolded about the tragic death of twenty young children and six staff members at Sandy Hook Elementary School in December 2012. Within a few days, several packs of comfort dogs arrived on the scene in Connecticut to try to ease the pain and provide some relief from the incomprehensible stress the entire community was experiencing. Lutheran Church Charities, K-9's for Kids Pediatric Therapy Dogs, and the Hudson Valley Golden Retrievers Club were just a few of the official canine compassion groups who came to offer whatever relief they could. Images of children with tears transformed into smiles, even for only a moment, as they were greeted by wagging tails and canine kisses reminded everyone that, at least in these encounters, the potential for some kind of recovery following inexplicable tragedy does exist.

Healing dogs again came when called after the bombing at the Boston Marathon in April 2013. Some of the same dogs, who helped those in Newtown to process their grief, walked the halls of hospitals in Boston where the survivors of the bombing were recovering from this horrible tragedy. Two of the dogs, Addie and Maggie, arrived directly from Newtown where they had been working for four months.[52] Thirteen other dogs arrived from the North Shore Animal League, a dog rescue group, to provide some much needed "puppy love" at the Boston Medical Center.

The same kind of powerful moments occurred with dogs and first responders in the wake of the September 11 tragedies. Some of the dogs and handlers who responded that day were from the National Disaster Search Dog Foundation, an organization whose mission is to make sure "no one is left behind."[53] Other teams came from the areas close to New York City and arrived by the evening of September 11. All told there were over 400 dogs that came to the site of the collapsed World Trade Center, hoping to find survivors, but finally tasked with finding the remains of those who had died. Finding human remains is not an easy job for the dogs: they are trained to find live humans, and the death toll at the site was exhausting for them. One twelve-year-old search and rescue dog found the remains of two firemen, curled up next to them, and would not move. It was more than the dog could take, and his handler knew it was time to take him home.[54] But many of these search dogs kept on working for days and weeks, recovering remains that could help bring closure to the families who lost loved ones in the tragedy. And, in addition to their search work, many of the dogs doubled as therapy dogs, lifting the spirits of the humans working at that tragic site.[55] Dogs can help to heal even the most broken heart.

The ways that dogs have healed humans over generations are far-ranging. From licking the wounds of plague sufferers to sitting next to a soldier suffering from post-traumatic stress syndrome to spurring their sedentary owners to take a walk, dogs have been priceless companions for humans in pain as long as they have traveled together. And, with scientific methods uncovering even more ways for dogs to partner with humans in health care, the old wisdom about the healing lick might contain more wisdom than ever imagined.

From their earliest days as partners in the hunt and then in the herd, to their role as companions in the afterlife, and

Figure 6
A search and rescue dog with handler. Courtesy of Federal Emergency Management Agency. Photo by Andrea Booher, FEMA News Photo.

then as healing companions, dogs bring to the dog-human relationship moments that uplift both species—making them stronger, more productive, more complete. It is a road that, arguably, neither could have traveled alone. Humans and dogs enabled each other to make the journey. But that is not the whole story. There are also some more tragic and painful aspects of the interspecies partnership, ones that reveal how complicated the human-dog story actually is.

Chapter 4

- - - - - - - - -

Canines and Conquest
Invasion, Empire, and Dogs of War

*The capability they [the dogs] bring to the fight cannot be
replicated by man or machine. By all measures of perfor-
mance, their yield outperforms any asset we have in our
industry. Our Army would be remiss if we failed to invest
more in this incredibly valuable resource.*

—*General David Petraeus*[1]

As word hit the press about the capture of Osama bin Laden
in early May 2011, one particularly intriguing, mysterious,
and, for some, unexpected hero made the headlines. Apparently a military war dog (MWD) was part of the Navy SEAL
unit charged with the dangerous, important task of capture,
and this highly trained dog took an active part in the raid
on the building in Pakistan where bin Laden had been hiding.[2] For national security reasons, information about the
team who captured the terrorist was kept confidential. But
eventually the hero dog's identity was confirmed—his name is
"Cairo," U.S. Navy SEAL Team Six Dog, a highly trained Belgian Malinois. The war dog was equipped with a specialized
vest to protect him from bullets and even had a headphone

inserted in his ear so he could hear the whispered commands of his handler. The military team emphasized the necessity of having a military dog on the mission; Cairo was central to the operation. He was trained to pick up the scent of a particular individual (bin Laden). He could positively find and identify the target and could also serve as a distraction in the heat of battle. After an intense flight, something certainly not lost on Cairo, the helicopter landed, though not without incident—it hit a wall in the target compound. But Cairo kept his composure and executed the mission. It was successful. This military war dog, along with his team, exited with the target in hand. Osama bin Laden was dead, and Cairo became a hero.[3]

In light of this victory, Cairo received special military recognition and was even honored by the U.S. president, Barack Obama, in an official (albeit private to continue to protect the identities of the human soldiers) ceremony for the entire Navy team that captured the terrorist.[4] But his story was not happening in a void, he was not the only hero. Cairo was one of approximately 600 MWDs serving with the U.S. military in Afghanistan. As the dogs' handlers and other soldiers readily declare, the canines have saved countless lives. They are weapons with "hearts, minds, and souls."[5]

For some people, hearing the news about Cairo, this hero dog, marked the first time they really understood the significant role of dogs in war. Cairo served his nation well by assisting in capturing the person labeled by his country as the most notorious and wanted terrorist in the world. This military war dog was, indeed, a hero, and his nation was proud of his service, as they should have been. Little did many of those people watching the general news stories of this amazing event know that Cairo was not a new phenomenon. The dog-human-war alliance has played out on battlefields for thousands of years, as a central component in conflicts and conquests of myriad forms that occurred for various reasons: some good, others bad, almost all tragic in some way.

But on that scary, dark, violent night, Cairo did his job, the one his handler human had asked him to do and the one he had trained for, over the course of years. He performed an amazing service as a member of the U.S. Navy SEAL unit. Cairo revealed, yet again, that humans and dogs not only partner in the hunt and the herd, in healing and in death, but also in conquest and battle. The partnership is not always one that humans want to acknowledge; it bears war wounds for both species. But this unique interspecies relationship reflects, in painful and tragic ways, who humans sometimes are and who humans at times have been, in many complicated chapters of history. It also reveals who dogs are and have been— faithful and brave, trusting humans as the ones who know what is best, willingly risking their lives to fulfill the task that humans ask them to do. Examining ways that humans work with dogs in war, conquest, and invasion points to amazing feats of mutual heroism and selflessness, but it can also raise questions about how cultures have wielded power, conquered others, and left a bloody trail in their wake, including the blood of the dogs serving by their side.

Military War Dogs

One of the first scenes of the Oscar award–winning movie "The Gladiator" shows the central character—Maximus Decimus Meridius, portrayed by Russell Crowe—leading the Roman troops into the fray of battle astride his war horse. But the soldier who is actually in front of the imperial forces as they charge the enemy is not this mighty general but a large dog, as would likely have been the case for a Roman battalion with its massive canine soldiers. Just as the familiar image of a guard dog replete with a spiked collar and

identified by the phrase "Cave Canem" graces the entrance
to a Roman house in Pompeii, large dogs greeted the enemies
of Rome on battlefields throughout the Mediterranean world
and northwestern Europe for centuries. Romans frequently
scouted for new, useful types of dogs as they moved into and
conquered other lands and people. They were particularly
fond of some of the dogs they encountered on the British
Isles, for example, and a specific trade in these hounds grew
quickly. Romans commemorated their dogs of war and conquest in works of art that reveal their significance for Roman
culture and power.[6]

But the Roman Empire was not the first to discover the
military value of dogs. For at least the last four thousand
years dogs have occupied a central role in human military
ventures. Some of the earliest evidence goes back to the Mesopotamian world where references to dogs and their handlers
are found in army records.[7] One very early reference is to the
"K-9 Corps" of the ancient Third Dynasty of Ur (c. 2100–
2000 BCE). These dog teams guarded high-status people,
among other jobs, and were occasionally portrayed following chariots into battle. In some instances the handlers of the
dogs were ranked just below generals in the military hierarchy, a fact that elevates the grade of the Mesopotamian army
dogs significantly. Other intriguing evidence consists of docu-
ments that list other animals, mostly equines, needed to feed
the dogs.[8] As a matter of fact, at that particular time in Ur,
since access to food is counted as an indicator, dogs and some
people held a similar status, each receiving the same rations
of the same types of food.[9] The K-9 Corps of the Ur dynasty
obviously warranted such an investment of resources.

Other ancient evidence of empire-building dogs shows
up in scores of iconographical pieces. One of the most spec-
tacular images of war dogs is on a painted chest found in
the tomb of King Tutankhamun of Egypt, who ruled in the

fourteenth century BCE. Here dogs are depicted running beside the chariot of the pharaoh as he heads into battle, bow and arrow drawn.[10] Ancient Egyptians were attracted to dogs not only as symbols of the afterlife and as adept hunters but also as tools of power for the building of empire.

On the heels of the age of the dog-revering Egyptian's domination of a large portion of the Mediterranean, but before the dog-savvy (and canine assisted) Roman Empire conquered the area, various Hellenistic and Persian cultures took control—also with dogs at hand. Dogs were central to many of these cultural systems—as herders of goats, sentries at home, exterminators of pests, and important figures in mythology. An additional service they provided was acting as partners in conquest. Used in various, creative ways to aid in battle, dogs were significant and powerful comrades. During his invasion of Egypt in 525 BCE, for example, Cambyses II placed dogs at the front of the military line. Because the Egyptians recognized them as sacred animals, they ceased using some of their most powerful weapons against the Persians. Cambyses knew that his enemy would likely recoil at the idea of killing the dogs, and his plan worked. The Persians won that battle, opening the way for their forces to invade Egypt.[11] And he was not the only one to employ dogs in a somewhat passive assistance in warfare. The widely hailed Darius the Great (550–486 BCE) used a diversionary tactic to deceive the enemy. When he decided to retreat from a losing battle, Darius left dogs in the camp. Because of the barking canines, along with braying mules also left behind, the foe failed to realize that Darius and his army had left until after they were out of reach. In this case, dogs were among those used as tools, but then abandoned during warfare, likely becoming casualties of human battle.[12]

Numerous other sources indicate the use of dogs by Hellenistic powers.[13] As we have seen, Alexander the Great was accompanied into battle by a loyal dog, Peritas, who died while they were on a military expedition and was given a full military burial. And when Hannibal crossed the Alps, in 218 BCE, he not only had elephants with him, but large Rottweiler-like dogs. Other Greek commanders used dogs in various ways to win battles and conquer others—both their neighbors and those more far-flung. For example the Roman historian Aelian (2nd century CE) described dogs accompanying the Magnesians when they fought the Ephesians:

> [Among] the *Magnetes* who border upon *Mæander* warring against the *Ephesians*, every Horseman took along with him a Hound, and a Servant that served as an Archer. As soon as they came near, the Dogs falling fiercely upon the Enemy, disordered them, and the Servants advancing before their Masters, shot. The Dogs first routed them, then the Servants did them much harm.[14]

As the horse-mounted warriors rode in battle, each with a dog, they would send the canines rushing forward to cause confusion before hurling their spears. No doubt, many dogs were lost in these moments of mayhem with projectiles flying.

So when the Roman Empire employed large dogs in battle, they were following a well-established tradition. It is likely that Greeks and Romans used Molossian-type dogs in battle. This ancient breed, the ancestor of mastiffs and other large dogs including Rottweilers and Great Danes, is mentioned in a number of Roman texts.[15] The Roman poet Grattius (first century CE) mentions these large dogs specifically, "when serious work has come, when bravery must be shown, and the impetuous War-god calls in the utmost hazard," the "renowned Molossians" were put to work.[16] Some of these dogs were acquired from the Celtic people whom the Romans had already conquered. Both continental Celts in Gaul and those at the edges of Europe in Scotland and Ireland had large dogs who guarded their homes and fought beside them as they defended their territory against Roman invasion. Even the famous St. Patrick mentions the trade of large Irish dogs in his *Confession.*[17]

As the Roman period waned and other European dynasties arose, the practice of using dogs in war continued. One remarkable piece of evidence indicating the significance of canine warriors is the gorgeous Bayeux Tapestry which tells the story of William the Conqueror's Norman invasion of England in 1066 (a turning point in European history). Thirty-five dogs appear in this visual depiction of the battle. They charge into the fight in front of or under the feet of the horse-mounted armies. The dogs pictured here are large and usually dressed in heavy chain collars. War dogs had become not only a tool, but a tradition.

While the myriad individual stories of dogs in battle are too numerous to tell, several particularly touching accounts of military dogs come from the tragic period of the nineteenth-century Civil War in the United States.[18] One of these dogs was named "Jack," and he served with the 102nd Pennsylvania Volunteers Regiment from 1861 to 1864. During this time he was even held as a prisoner of war for six months in Virginia, though he was eventually traded back to his unit in exchange for a Confederate soldier. According to reports, Jack would search out injured soldiers on the battlefield, respond to bugle calls, and enter into the fray of battle—he was wounded several times. Sadly, he disappeared in a battle and his regiment never discovered what happened to him.[19]

Another famous Civil War dog, Sallie, is commemorated at Gettysburg, one of the most significant battle sites of the war (figure 7). Sallie's connection to the 11th Pennsylvania Infantry started when she was four weeks old and was presented as a gift to Lieutenant William Terry. Sallie

Figure 7
Sallie, a famous Civil War dog, is commemorated on a monument at
Gettysburg. © 2012 R. G. Blakeslee, www.nycivilwar.us.

accompanied the unit in battles from 1862 until her death in 1865. She saw some of the most horrific fights in the war— Antietam, Fredericksburg, Chancellorsville, and Gettysburg. At that last battle, when her regiment was forced to retreat, Sallie was lost in the chaos. Three days later her regiment found her again.Sallie had not left their original position and was still guarding the bodies of her fallen comrades. This heroic dog was shot in the head and killed on the battlefield in Hatchers Run, Virginia. In 1890 the survivors of the regiment commissioned a monument to be erected at Gettysburg memorializing the 11th Pennsylvania Infantry. At the base of the monument is a statue of Sallie, lying at the feet of those soldiers to whom she was so dedicated in life and in death.[20]

Though Russia, Germany, France, and Great Britain all had official war dog training programs during World War I, the United States did not. But even this official stance could not stop Stubby, a pit bull mix who was found by Private Robert Conroy while he was training at Yale University in 1917. Stubby's military buddies smuggled him onto the ship, and supposedly hid him in a coal bin, when they were deployed to Europe, so the squatty dog was headed into battle (figure 8). Not only did he quickly learn to alert the troops to attacks such as incoming mustard gas, he also became a comfort dog for soldiers convalescing after injuries. Because of his valiant effort to capture a German soldier by biting him on the legs until the U.S. soldiers arrived, Stubby was promoted to sergeant, thus becoming the first dog in the U.S. military to be given a rank. Following the war, he met at least two U.S. presidents and, sporting his blanket covered with medals, led troops in victory parades.[21]

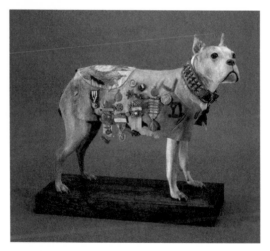

Figure 8
Stubby was prepared by taxidermists to be on display in "The Price of Freedom: Americans At War" exhibit at the National Museum of American History. Photo courtesy of Armed Forces History, Smithsonian Institution. Armed Forces History, Division of History of Technology, National Museum of American History.

By the time World War II hit, the United States jumped onto the war dog bandwagon. Having seen the success of war dogs with units from allied countries in World War I, and even with unofficial dogs like Stubby serving in the U.S. military, a call went out for volunteer dogs following the attack on Pearl Harbor in 1942. In response to that plea, "Dogs for Defense" was organized and people started to enlist their pet dogs in the military for training.[22] While not all these dogs made it through boot camp, many did and they headed to the front lines.

Particularly in the Pacific theater, where dense jungle terrains required different kinds of military tactics, dogs proved very useful on the front lines as scouts and sentries. Caesar, a German shepherd, became a figurehead and a hero for his actions during the campaign on Bougainville, one of the large Solomon Islands. His Marine battalion was trapped by hostile fire, and their radio had failed. So Caesar "made nine runs under fire between the unit and its command post" in order to deliver essential communications. Then, when a Japanese soldier attempted to throw a grenade into the foxhole with Caesar's handler, the brave dog attacked and suffered war injuries. For this the dog was promoted to sergeant, albeit unofficially.[23]

Similar reports from the period indicate that military war dogs saved lives by detecting bombs, alerting to enemy advances, moving information, and offering solace, yet in some ways it is hard to quantify their direct impact. But for one group of military dogs, those with the Arctic Search and Rescue Units, the numbers are recorded. During World War II, pilots flew over the Arctic to make the connection between Canada and the United States and their European allies. Flying in these conditions was not easy, and many planes went down in the cold, forbidding north. It seemed impossible to retrieve the surviving soldiers and the remains of those who perished.

But there was one way to get to these heroes—dogsled teams. So the United States established the "War Dog Reception and Training Center" in Rimini, Montana. Here some eight hundred sled dogs and their military handlers trained for the worst possible scenarios, rescuing downed pilots and recovering equipment in the deadly Arctic terrain. It was not easy to find people who knew how to work with dog teams, or to find dogs who were up to the task.[24] Units of dogs and handlers were positioned along the Arctic flyways so they could respond quickly. These teams would then deploy to a downed plane and evacuate the soldiers, equipment, and supplies. Over the course of their service, the Arctic Search and Rescue Units brought out at least 150 survivors, 300 casualties, and "millions of dollars worth of equipment."[25] This program focused entirely on saving lives. A poignant statement from one of the soldiers stationed at Rimini points to ways the sled dogs offered a hopeful side to the tragedy of war: "We were privileged to be participating in a process of saving lives rather than taking them. In wartime, this is a rare privilege."[26]

At the end of World War II, war dogs were firmly planted in U.S. military planning and culture. From that point forward calls would not go out for canine volunteers to enlist, rather specific dog breeds were selected—German shepherds, Belgian Malinois, Doberman pinschers, and several others. While the impact of dogs, particularly in the Pacific, was widely acknowledged, ambivalence about dogs as soldiers and even a hint of cynicism remained. This was evident in stories about these dogs reported in popular publications like the *Saturday Evening Post*, which asked the question, "Have the War Dogs Been Good Soldiers?" The article opened by criticizing the "gaudy specifications" and "highly colored exaggerations of Rover's niche in the war effort" and concluded with a summary that confirmed the official position of the military—dogs are equipment, not soldiers:

What you've seen about decorations being awarded to dogs, however, is strictly a myth. The armed forces still confine that brand of commendation to men. For meritorious services, Rover got a pat on the head, maybe an extra chunk of meat, and the rather rare opportunity to bite a general.[27]

This overt subordinate status of dogs in the U.S. military would follow the canine soldiers into the Vietnam War with tragic consequences.

But there were definitely veterans of World War II who did not forget the service of their dog comrades. The United States Military Cemetery on Guam witnesses this remembrance through a poignant War Dog Memorial, even though it took fifty years to get the memorial placed on the island. The majority of the dogs who served on Guam during World War II were Doberman pinschers. These dogs led over 550 patrols on the island, and twenty-five of the dogs died during their military service there.[28] Inscribed on the memorial is this touching tribute:

> 25 Marine War Dogs gave their lives liberating Guam in 1944. They served as sentries, messengers, scouts. They explored caves, detected mines and booby traps.
>
> —SEMPER FIDELIS

> Given in their memory and on behalf of the surviving men of the 2nd and 3rd marine war dog platoons, many of whom owe their lives to the bravery and sacrifice of these gallant animals.

The memorial is placed close to where these twenty-five dogs were buried by their handlers.

Well before the U.S. military officially recognized the service of dogs in war, the British military made it a regular practice by presenting the Dickin Medal (often equated with the Victoria Cross, Britain's highest military honor for valor) to war animals from the middle of World War II. One of the most amazing recipients of that award was Judy, a pointer born in Shanghai in 1937. Judy had served as a mascot on several British navy ships when one of them, the *HMS Grasshopper*, was torpedoed. Along with the crew and passengers of the ship, Judy swam to safety on an island in the Pacific Ocean. Reportedly, she saved her shipwrecked comrades by digging for fresh water on the uninhabited island. But her saga did not end there. She remained with the soldiers as they tried to get to safety, only to be captured by the Japanese army. Judy was a prisoner of war for three years at the Gloergoer camp. Here, she protected her fellow prisoners by alerting them to scorpions and snakes and by trying to protect them from the enemy guards. At this POW camp, Judy met up with Frank Williams, a British aircraftsman; these two friends would stick together for the rest of Judy's life. When the prisoners were transferred in 1944, Williams snuck Judy aboard the ship in a rice sack. After the ship was torpedoed, Williams thought he had lost his beloved war dog until he heard from other soldiers about a dog who had helped them survive at sea. He knew it had to be Judy, and, shortly thereafter, she turned up again in Williams' new POW camp. Over the course of their time in this camp, Judy was sentenced to death and attacked by an alligator. But she survived, and, in the process, kept Williams and the other prisoners hopeful. Later, Williams said that Judy "saved his life in so many ways . . . the greatest way of all was giving me a reason to live."[29] When the war was over Judy returned to Great Britain with Williams, and, even though she had to go through six months of quarantine, she emerged as a national hero and received the Dickin Medal in 1946.[30]

Treatment of war dogs has been and remains a controversial topic in the United States, though less so in some European countries where war dogs have been honored with medals of valor and official memorials. While some people think these canine troops should be recognized with medals and honors, and should be treated with dignity following their service, others see this recognition as a slighting of the service of humans in the military. This conflict came to a head during and immediately following the Vietnam War. By almost all accounts, dogs working in the U.S. military were instrumental in the controversial Southeast Asian conflict. Over 4,000 dogs were deployed, and, by all accounts, they saved the lives of hundreds of U.S. troops. These dogs were trackers, sentries, scouts, and even tunnel rats (sent into tunnels to look for explosives or for hidden combatants). But at the end of the Vietnam War, the dogs, who were classified as military equipment, were left behind. There they were either euthanized or transferred to the South Vietnamese army. When their handlers returned home, some of them fought for this new cause—reclassifying the dogs so they could be adopted instead of abandoned.[31] Still, it took until the year 2000 for a military dog adoption law to pass.

While most military war dogs have been used as a form of defense—searching out explosive devices, acting as sentries or guards—not as many have been used as offensive weapons. But there are times when dogs have been deployed in this way. Some of the mastiffs used by the Greek, Persian, and Roman armies were used to attack, and, in the modern period, both Russia and Israel have trained dogs as offensive weapons.[32] One troubling report from World War II described the Russian Army using dogs as a "mobile variant of the Molotov cocktail." These dogs, equipped with an explosive pack, were trained to move between the treads of Nazi tanks in order to destroy the vehicle. As a contemporary newspiece described the tactic, as well as the reaction of the Russian war dog handler, "The guerrilla feels very bad about Fedor, but he feels very good about the tank."[33] Other uses of dogs being trained to attack combatants directly, which is akin to some of the work that K-9 police units are trained to perform, are widely criticized by animal activist and humane organizations. Dog behaviorists also suggest that it is an unnatural and highly destructive way to train dogs, since it is against this domesticated canine's nature to attack humans. Luckily for humans and dogs, it is a maneuver rarely deployed.

"Rebecca's War Dog of the Week" is a column in *Foreign Policy* magazine. Each article focuses on a different canine soldier or related issue. The December 14, 2012, column told the story of Tygo, a four-year-old Irish setter. Tygo was a Specialized Search Dog whose job was to search out explosive devices in Afghanistan. On November 10, 2012, he was killed by an IED (improvised explosive device) while on duty. Other stories tell of happier endings, with a soldier and handler retiring from the service together, or of a military war dog who lived out the rest of his or her life peacefully and then died from old age. But those are mixed with tragic stories like Tygo's—a dog who did what he was asked and died a violent death at a young age.

Life as a war dog is obviously not easy, even if a dog is one of the survivors. Many war dogs die in battle, but others live bearing tragic war scars, emotional and physical. By the time of the wars in Iraq and Afghanistan, policies had changed, so that—unlike in the Vietnam War era—U.S. military war dogs could come back home after their service ended; but some of them suffered from the incredible stress of the situations to which they had been exposed. Now there is an official name for their ailment: canine post-traumatic stress disorder. The Daniel E. Holland Military Working Dog Hospital at Lackland Air Force Base in San Antonio sees many of these cases. It is estimated that 5 percent of MWDs suffer from canine

PTSD. Some of the dogs are able to be treated and then return to active duty, others are retired.[34] But they, like the humans with whom they work, begin to connect their work with danger and fear. A war theater can be as traumatic for a dog as for a person.

And even with the recognition of these disorders, and hopeful avenues for treatment of them, sometimes the dogs are still deemed too dangerous after their military service to become pets. As recently as 2012 the British military encountered significant pushback when it was revealed that they had decided to euthanize over 800 war dogs between 2002 and 2012. These dogs had all served in Iraq and Afghanistan. When they returned, it was determined that they could not be rehomed. Some members of Parliament and animal welfare groups were outraged. But, as the Ministry of Defense claimed, retraining was ineffective for many of the dogs.[35] It was the price the dogs paid for their military service.

Reading through the Military Working Dogs Facebook page offers incredible, poignant, and troubling moments. Touching tributes celebrate the bravery and comradeship of dogs, particularly those serving in Iraq and Afghanistan. Dogs are pictured being lowered from helicopters, training to detect explosive devices, standing alongside their human trainers. They are also memorialized. MWD Bak, U.S. Army, was killed in action in Afghanistan; he was 3½ years old (October 9, 2009–March 11, 2013). On May 14, 2013, at Wright Army Airfield in Georgia, an official "Memorial Service (combat death)" was held for Bak. This turnaround in recognition of the work of these dogs is a major cultural shift from the Vietnam War era, though in many ways it is simply a return to the days of Alexander the Great: humans recognizing and honoring the dogs who serve in these most violent of our interactions with each other.

Blood and Hounds

. . . now we were overtaken, and torn to pieces by the terrible bloodhound.

—*Frederick Douglass*[36]

In 1847 Frederick Douglass, an amazing orator and leader of the abolition movement, after traveling to Ireland and England, offered a farewell address to the British people. In this speech Douglass harshly critiques the continuing atrocity of slavery in America and implicates the terrifying use of dogs in his imagery:

> This clause of the American constitution makes the whole land one vast hunting-ground for men: it gives to the slave-holder the right at any moment to set his well-trained bloodhounds upon the track of the poor fugitive; hunt him down like a wild beast, and hurl him back to the jaws of slavery, from which he had, for a brief space of time, escaped.[37]

Of course, Douglass knew firsthand about being hunted down and captured since he was an escaped slave himself. The history of the use of dogs as tools of conquest and domination is the shadowy side of their history as heroes in war. While war dogs serve their handlers faithfully and sometimes die in the process, the same keen canine abilities to track and hunt have been used as weapons of violence by conquerors and masters against humans who are being oppressed and enslaved.

Over the course of several centuries, the European invasion and conquering of the Americas marked one of the most appalling, indeed deadly, episodes of the human-dog partnership. The various ways dogs were used as tools of war by European powers damaged the canine-human companion and ally relationship for centuries. Recalling that dogs accompanied the first humans who migrated to North and South America thousands of years ago, one can see the scope of the tragedy. When humans and dogs first crossed the Bering land bridge, dogs were the only domesticated species shared by all humans globally, and also the only domesticated animal species in the Americas. They were partnering with the earliest human inhabitants of the Americas as hunters, as draft animals, and as pets.[38] Over the course of millennia, native North and South Americans were ritually burying dogs, pondering their significance in myths and legends, and working side-by-side with them in hunting.

Eventually, unique breeds of dogs, such as the Mexican and Peruvian hairless types, were developed and adapted for very specific tasks. For example, the Fuegian dog, who some early anthropologists refer to as "canoe" dogs, adapted as otter hunters.[39] These stocky, strong dogs could easily be retrieved into canoes from the water and served as invaluable co-workers.[40] A whole taxonomy of American dogs finally developed as archaeologists began examining, at least in some basic ways, remains of ancient dogs. Different types of dogs included Eskimo, Plains Indian, Mexican hairless, Inca, Klamath Indian, and more.[41] Unfortunately, by the time significant interest focused on trying to understand and document this complex and long-standing relationship, most indigenous dog types disappeared. Regardless, there was— and in many cases still is—a strong, bonded, human-dog relationship in the Americas from the earliest years of human habitation in the Western Hemisphere.

Tragically, much of this changed when European conquerors flooded the Americas. The invaders were, too often, accompanied and assisted by well-trained dogs, who were very different from the native dogs of the Americas. Mastiffs and hounds, bred for military and hunting purposes for centuries, traveled in the seafaring vessels with conquistadors, slave-traders, and priests. From that point forward, and for obvious reasons, dogs morphed into a symbol of empire and destruction for Native Americans throughout the hemisphere. Bartolomé de Las Casas (1484–1566) captured the essence of the fear instilled by the Spanish conquerors and their use of dogs in his account of the destruction of the West Indies, "As has been said, the Spaniards train their fierce dogs to attack, kill and tear to pieces the Indians."[42] The canine companion became the canine of conquest.

But the use of dogs as tools of power and destruction did not stop with the initial centuries of encounter. Dogs continued to be used to push people into submission. The Second Seminole War (1835–1842) is a telling and horrid example of the violent ways dogs were employed in the Americas, both with indigenous populations and with African slaves,[43] and their role in that tragedy. In 1821 the United States finalized its contested acquisition of Florida from the original Spanish invaders. At that point a section of central Florida was designated as a reservation for the Seminoles and other Native American groups, including Creeks, Alabamas, and Choctaws, still living in the territory. While this fact alone bred tension, there was an additional issue that angered U.S. government officials. Some slaves from plantations bordering Florida found sanctuary with the Native Americans, including on the reservation land. Then, in 1830, the Indian Removal Act was passed by Congress, with intense pressure from the newly elected president Andrew Jackson. This act allowed for the forcible relocation of all Native Americans living east of the Mississippi River to lands west of that river. One of the many resulting conflicts was the Second Seminole War, also known as the War for Florida or Bloodhound War. It was the final major military fight between the United States and the Native American inhabitants of Florida.[44]

Dogs played a significant role in the Bloodhound War, hence this alternative name for the conflict. For decades preceding this conflagration, tracking dogs had been imported to the United States from places such as Cuba that specialized in breeding scent hounds in order to find runaway slaves. Many of these dogs had been developed by the Spanish as part of their program to conquer Central and South America. The English name "bloodhound" was first used to refer to these dogs in the late eighteenth century, as part of a campaign to criticize the British government for using this "atrocious" mode of warfare in Jamaica.[45] In other words, the designation was a pejorative one used to condemn the way that people were using these dogs to subjugate other people, both in the Caribbean and in the U.S. system of slavery.[46] But the name stuck, and for some quite appropriate reasons. While the tracking dogs themselves were likely not the ones actually to attack people, they most certainly were the tools to locate slaves who were trying to gain their freedom.

It was with this historical baggage that the tracking dogs accompanied the U.S. military into the Second Seminole War. One contemporary image tells the story as fully as any verbal description. "Hunting Indians in Florida with Blood Hounds" portrays Zachary Taylor, who would later be president of the U.S., on horseback pursuing retreating Seminoles.[47] Taylor, the commander of U.S. forces in Florida at the time, is astride his horse, but more importantly here he is accompanied by tracking dogs. One dog is injured on the ground at the feet of Taylor's horse, but another is lunging at the neck of an adult man who is shielding a woman and a child from the vicious canine. Taylor victoriously exclaims, "Hurra! Captain, we've got them at last, the dogs are at them—now forward with the Rifle and Bayonet and 'give them Hell Brave Boys,' let not a red nigger escape,—show no mercy, exterminate them,—this day we'll close the Florida War, and write its history in the blood of the Seminole." It is a gruesome, horrible image that reflects both the terrifying actuality and propaganda associated with dogs, imperialism, slavery, and conquest.

With this history of using tracking dogs to thwart the efforts of slaves to escape to freedom, and to force eviction of Native Americans from their land, it is no wonder that by the 1950s and 1960s, at the height of the civil rights movement in the U.S., images of police with K-9s attacking nonviolent protestors prompted such strong responses. In his seminal piece, "Letter from Birmingham Jail," Martin Luther King Jr. makes direct reference to the use of police dogs: "You warmly commended the Birmingham police force for keeping 'order' and 'preventing violence.' I doubt that you would have so warmly commended the police force if you had seen its dogs sinking their teeth into unarmed, nonviolent Negroes."[48] When dogs—who for over 15,000 years have befriended and lived with humans on every continent, to their mutual benefit—are turned from friend into foe, the resulting horror is particularly appalling.

Dogs as symbols of empire occurred globally, however, not just in the violent encounters between the European colonial powers and the inhabitants of North and South America. For example, one of the ways that Japan created imperial aspirations in the late nineteenth and early twentieth century involved carefully constructed use of dogs. Over a short period of time, as Japan emerged as a geopolitical force, indigenous dog breeds became symbols of its power and of its unique status—as a nation in East Asia that was not a European colony but one, rather, that had colonies of its own. By the 1930s, on the eve of World War II, the Japanese codified and nationalized dogs as part of creating their own imperial identity.[49]

In the mid-1930s, in between the two world wars but still at the height of the global British Empire, the *Illustrated London News* published a book with a compelling and revealing title: *"A Dog Map of the World": The Countries of Origin of Some Seventy Breeds of Domesticated Dogs, Half of Them Evolved in the British Isles!*[50] In many ways, the final exclamation point tells the story of imperial identity—not only did the sun never set on the British Empire, but it never set on its dogs either.

Conquering Other Species

The human dimensions of the violent use of dogs are potent and scary, but there are other dimensions as well. As a pervasive, arguably even invasive, species, humans have taken over the planet. In some places and times, humans accomplished this with dogs on our heels and at our command. Humans and dogs were and are, literally, coinvasive species. As humans expanded geographically from Africa into Eurasia, then into the Pacific islands and the Americas, an interesting phenomenon occurred—the major megafauna (large native animals) on those newly inhabited continents disappeared.[51] Sub-Saharan Africa, where humans and the large animals lived together for millennia prior to the domestication of animals and the development of powerful weapons, is the only large landmass where megafauna were not driven to extinction. But on the other continents, where humans arrived with tools and with dogs, other large land animals were generally destroyed. While the direct cause of this mass extinction might never be fully determined, certainly the human-dog hunting team worked against countless native animals.[52]

It is still the case today that dogs, when humans take them into sensitive ecosystems, can have a negative impact on indigenous species. Isolated islands are some of the most easily studied systems where invasive species' impact becomes readily apparent. For example, the Channel Islands off the coast of California witnessed the introduction of dogs, along with their human companions, at least 6,000 years ago (and possibly as long as 10,000 years ago).[53] On these isolated islands, dogs and humans existed in a close relationship, evidenced by ritual burial of dogs on several of the islands. But this partnership proved destructive to native species, particularly during breeding seasons. And dogs may well have contributed to the extinction of such species as the flightless goose. Invading together, humans and dogs can be very destructive. Eventually dogs transported by European settlers who raised sheep on the islands replaced the Native Americans' dogs, introducing yet another invasive species (the sheep) to the sensitive space. When the overall impact of dogs became apparent, they were removed from all but one of the islands.[54]

A contemporary critical case of this coinvasion of humans and dogs is the Galapagos Islands off the coast of Ecuador. Famous for their connection to Charles Darwin's ideas about evolution, the Galapagos Islands were relatively free of human (and accompanying dog) habitation until the middle of the nineteenth century. But over the course of 150 years, the impact of humans and dogs has been dramatic.[55] In 1832 General José Villamil took dogs with him when he first settled one of the islands, and they accompanied him, of course, when he went to another island. This general apparently left dogs on several of the islands, abandoning them there to fend for themselves. So by the end of the nineteenth century, there were groups of feral dogs roaming, and scientists noted large-scale destruction of tortoise eggs.[56] While dogs are not the only culprit—cats, horses, rats, goats, pigs play their parts—they are a major one. By the early twenty-first century, only four of the original fifteen subspecies of the giant tortoise survive on the Galapagos. The tortoises, along with other vulnerable species, particularly those who nested in the ground, fell prey to stray or otherwise roaming dogs.[57]

So while there are myriad instances of dogs and humans as mutually beneficial and even caring partners, in the conquest of people and land this powerful relationship fueled pain and destruction. Dogs have been tools of empire and oppression, as well as partners in the invasion of myriad ecosystems. In these cases, the ugly, horrid, tragic chapters in the history of the human-dog partnership must be considered as part of the millennia-long struggle of some humans seeking power over other humans—and over the entire planet. In this saga, the dog is something of an unwilling or at least an unintentional player, but still involved in the destruction.

A Hopeful Coda

To balance this abuse of dogs by human conquerors, there have been times when dogs appeared as, or were at least interpreted to be, active resistors against empire, war, and terror. In his essay "The Name of a Dog, or Natural Rights," Emmanuel Levinas, a twentieth-century philosopher who grappled with human-animal identity, focused on two rarely cited passages from the biblical book of Exodus:

> "You shall be people consecrated to me; therefore you shall not eat any meat that is mangled by beasts in the field; you shall throw it to the dogs." (Exodus 22:31)

> "Not a dog shall growl at any of the Israelites—not at people, not at animals—so that you may know that the LORD makes a distinction between Egypt and Israel."
> (Exodus 11:6)

Moses is the speaker in these passages, he tells the Israelites not to fear barking dogs who could warn Pharoah of their escape from captivity in Egypt. And, as Moses claims, the dogs maintain their silence, thus proving that they are acting as agents of the divine in this instance rather than as tools of the empire, of Pharoah. Because of that act of solidarity with the Israelites, many interpreters, Levinas included, claim that the meat mentioned in Exodus 22 is a reward for the dogs who were loyal to them.[58] In other words, the meat is not thrown to the dogs just because this particular meat is unclean and therefore unfit for human consumption, but primarily because the dogs deserve this as recognition of their service and faithfulness.

The philosopher does not stop there, because this story from Exodus reminds him of "Bobby," a dog whom he met in a Nazi prisoner of war camp. Here the tormented Jewish prisoners were, in the eyes of the Germans, "subhuman." In the midst of this horrid situation, "a wandering dog" joined the demoralized prisoners and, as Levinas states, gave some sense of meaning to them again:

> One day he came to meet this rabble as we returned under guard from work. . . . [W]e called him Bobby, an exotic name, as one does with a cherished dog. He would appear at morning assembly and was waiting for us as we returned, jumping up and down and barking in delight. For him there was no doubt that we were men.[59]

Levinas continues to call Bobby a "descendant of the dogs of Egypt." Whereas the Nazis treated the Jews like animals, the dog treated them humanely. Bobby's "friendly growling, his animal faith, was born from the silence of the forefathers on the banks of the Nile." The dog subverts the power of the empire, of the Nazis, by making the Jewish prisoners of war human again.

Chapter 5

- - - - - - - - - -

Dogs of Design
The Frankenstein Syndrome
in a Changing World

*[O]nce I falsely hoped to meet the beings who, pardoning
my outward form, would love me for the excellent qualities which I was capable of unfolding.*

— *Mary Shelley,* Frankenstein[1]

Stevie, the Wonder Dog, is a blind pit bull. This group of
dogs, pit bulls, is not actually a breed in the traditional sense
but a category that includes various breeds and mixtures.
Pit bulls are maligned, loved, abused, praised, outlawed,
chained, tortured, adored. Stevie breaks all of the negative
stereotypes associated with pit bulls, which is not a surprise
to the many humans who live with gentle and charming "pit-
ties." He was blind at birth, as were his two sisters, and all
three were dropped off at a shelter in Salt Lake City, Utah,
when they were five weeks old. Luckily for Stevie, a dog rescue volunteer with the Utah Animal Advocacy Foundation
noticed these three at-risk pups and pulled them out of the
shelter into a safe foster home.[2] Not only does Stevie have
a disability, but since he is a pit bull, whatever that might
mean, he is automatically feared and ostracized by many of

Figure 9
Stevie the Wonder Dog. Photo courtesy of Jen Milner.

the humans he encounters. So being rescued from the shelter was, in and of itself, a huge hurdle.

Fast-forward a few years to March 2011, and this beautiful, blind, male pit bull earned his designation as a certified therapy dog through the Delta Society program (figure 9).[3] Now Stevie spends time working with homeless and low-income people with drug or alcohol addictions. He is a kindred spirit, fighting against the odds and bravely facing adversity with them.[4] Like many of his maligned pit bull compatriots, Stevie defies expectations and changes lives in amazing, beautiful ways. In February 2012 Stevie even won the "National Pet Radio" contest sponsored by National Public Radio. The caption below his winning picture (which shows him taking pledges at his local radio station) reads, "This is Stevie the Wonder Dog taking pledges at his favorite NPR station, KCPW in Salt Lake City. Since Stevie is blind, he depends on NPR more than most for all of his news and information."[5] Stevie begs questions about who these dogs are, how they became cultural icons, what mixed messages they send, and how they simultaneously evoke terror and compassion.

Pit bulls are not the only dogs who find themselves stuck in the whirlwind of the human dog-breeding conundrum. From tiny teacup Chihuahuas whose skulls often lack the volume to contain their brains to massive Irish wolfhounds prone to heart disease and bloat, humans have shaped dogs to serve our particular needs and, in the process, created "monsters." Humans and dogs lived side-by-side for thousands of years before humans started to engage in intensive, selective breeding practices. There was certainly some selection, on both the part of the early humans and by proto-dogs breeding among themselves, thus dogs are no longer wolves. But starting a few thousand years ago, humans began to select for very particular traits. And in the last several hundred years, this practice of selection became aggressive and intense. Humans looked for very particular traits, often ones that were judged by appearance only, not utility, and in the process created genetic bottlenecks that are harmful for dogs and humans alike.

Mary Shelley's *Frankenstein: or the Modern Prometheus* helps shed light on the status of the pit bull and of other specific types of dogs formed by humans over the last several millennia. In this complicated, multilayered classic Gothic novel—familiar in popular culture, retold frequently, and reinterpreted countless times—Frankenstein, something of a scientist in the early nineteenth century, makes a Creature using the newly found power of electricity, to defy, or literally undo, death. The Creature, who remains unnamed in the novel, is not exactly what his creator imagined, and almost immediately Frankenstein seeks his death. There is likely no need to retell the tale here, as very few are unfamiliar with the story in some form. Its central themes are still debated: problems with the mortal (human) assuming the role of Creator/God; questions about viciousness as a learned, not an innate, behavior; ideas about who is a monster and why; questions about beings who are abhorred and love simultaneously; and so on.

Regardless of the endless deliberations over the theme of the novel, most agree that the story digs into the idea of humans as shapers of life in some form, and of humans as destroyers of the same lives they create. As a recent interpretation suggests, Mary Shelley portrayed the Creature as displaying both an instinct both for self-preservation and for compassion. This compassion leads the Creature to seek out relationships with people around him. But his appearance evokes fear and rejection. Rather than supporting him, the creator abandons him and fails in his most basic responsibility—to socialize and care for his creation.[6]

Enter the dog-human relationship to the Frankenstein-Creature story. For the first dozen or more millennia of shared lives and cultures, humans and dogs did simultaneously shape each other, but with little apparent intentionality from either actor. That is the provocative story of this interspecies journey—humans and dogs created each other through starts and stops, shared livelihoods and spaces, forming each other for thousands of years. It is important in this joint process to recall that dogs were the only domesticated species populating both the "Old World" (Europe/Asia/Africa) and the "New World" (North/South America) five centuries ago, when Europeans first invaded the Western Hemisphere.[7] In other words, dogs are the only other animal species with whom all humans were living, over time and space, up until five centuries ago. We are companion species.

Over these hundreds of generations most humans still lived in small-scale groups, functioning as generalists with relatively egalitarian social structures and shared tasks for survival. Dogs served as sentinels, hunting partners, and general companions for humans during the period approximately 11,000 years ago when developing cultures on most continents were basically similar to each other, feeding themselves by hunting animals and gathering plants.[8] And by that point humans and dogs had already been living together for, at the very least, several thousand years.

Eventually human cultures, certainly deeply impacted by dogs, grew more and more specialized, albeit in different ways depending on, among other things, geography. So dogs were healers, pets for the wealthy, and tools of empire in addition to their well-established roles as hunters and herders. The initial stages of this separation of duties among groups of humans derived from different groups of people developing distinctive food production systems. Those systems integrated domesticated animals as well. In addition, these more sedentary cultures eventually included increasingly rigid and obvious human hierarchical systems with specialists—such as warriors, kings, and record-keepers. Obviously, a wealth hierarchy also developed, leading eventually to empires.

Related directly to these increasingly complex specialized human social systems, dogs with specific characteristics were selected to fill particular roles. Granted, that explanation is a condensed version of a complicated history that happens in different ways in different times and places. But, in short, as humans specialized, so did the dogs they were selecting and breeding. In order to create dogs uniquely suited to fill their needs, humans began to breed them to be larger or smaller, shorter or faster. Thus dogs with the speed and agility to catch fast animals that they chased primarily by sight emerged in North Africa and the Middle East with their more open hunting grounds. By contrast, in the wooded areas of northern Europe, scent hounds were a more effective hunting companion, and so dogs who could track prey with their noses to the ground were preferred. The rugged terrain of the Middle East also required a different dog, with other physical and behavioral characteristics, to help herd the sheep and goats. In various places, a rising affluent class of rulers longed for small lapdogs as companions and healers, so the ancient small breeds such as the Maltese (Mediterranean) and the Pekingese (East Asian) came onto the scene. Over the course of thousands of years, niche dogs were selected for and by niche humans.

This entire system of selective breeding of dogs was exaggerated at certain points in history. For example, two thousand years ago in the Roman Empire, dogs used as weapons of war were bred to emphasize impressive size and strength. Thus the largest dogs were mated to each other, eventually creating breeds of mastiffs. These dogs can outweigh even the largest gray wolf by at least one hundred pounds. At the same time, the smallest dogs were selected over generations to create tiny lapdogs, some smaller, as adults, than even newborn wolves. In both cases, extreme size led to physical ailments. Larger dogs suffered from issues such as hip dysplasia and smaller ones from crowded teeth and other dental woes.

But the most exaggerated human-driven selective reproduction of dogs, the real explosion of dog breeds, started in the later Middle Ages in Europe and the Mediterranean world. This explosion finally reached its zenith in the Victorian era, the period in Great Britain following on the heels of the publication of Mary Shelley's *Frankenstein*. During this period of intensive human-controlled breeding, dogs become not only uniquely varied among species, but also genetically plagued.

The roots of this growth in dog breeding could already be seen in the late eighteenth century when the first dog breeds, at least as they are referenced in the modern West, were classified into increasingly formalized categories.[9] Dogs were by then often used in sport hunting, less in hunting for sustenance, since other animals had been domesticated to provide meat. These sport-hunting dogs were owned by the economically elite humans: they were a luxury. By the end of the eighteenth century, pedigrees were maintained for foxhounds, thus this hunting dog won the prize as the first defined "breed" in Britain.[10] At that point, dog breeding was still mostly the purview of the elite, but it was rapidly transforming into one of the markers of a growing middle class in Britain as well, much to the dismay of the upper class. This expansion of dog breeding, and thus the pet industry, was part of the nineteenth century "commercialization of leisure," and it became highly specialized over a relatively short period of time.[11] New "fanciers" of dog breeding began recording the lineage of their dogs, with just a few generations at the beginning, in order to give them validity. The status symbol of owning a dog with an identifiable family tree was one of the social markers of the middle class. Dogs were increasingly categorized into very specific breeds and groups. From that point forward some dogs were "mutts" while others were "purebred."

According to the Kennel Club of the United Kingdom, the first dog show was held in 1859. Sixty dogs were entered into this show, all sporting dogs, and classified into two groups—pointers and setters.[12] The idea spread like wildfire, and the 1863 dog show held at Chelsea included over one thousand entries.[13] A decade later the official Kennel Club was founded in order to regulate dog shows and to maintain a studbook. Perfecting specific breeds for competition in what became known as conformation had begun, though some of its negative side effects would not be recognized for years.

The Creator's Success—and Frankenstein's Failures

Among the species listed, the dog is clearly the one with the highest number of recognized diseases, with over 1,000 inherited conditions so far reported.[14]

It seems obvious to point out that scientific knowledge and processes change with time. In *Frankenstein*, the author is posing questions about the use of the most advanced scientific knowledge of that era to create and destroy life. Frankenstein

employs the recently discovered power of electricity to generate life in the body of the Creature that he assembled from
other bodies. While tempting to draw conclusions about the
tensions between nature and culture here, an equally valid
interpretation of the Frankenstein story is that it first cele-
brates the power of understanding certain natural processes
and "mastering" them, only to show that they are much more
complicated than originally assumed. The Creature does
come to life when the scientist masters the use of electricity.
But the human fails to see all of the potential pitfalls associated with the science. A central drawback is that the new
Creature needs to be integrated carefully and thoughtfully
into society. In other words, the creator must take responsibility for the Creature.

Dogs provide a unique window into this same failure to
see the possible weaknesses of the whole because of a fas-
cination with the parts. As mentioned previously, archaeological evidence shows that dogs are the most diverse species
that has ever lived on the earth.[15] They have long or dwarf
legs, rounded or elongated heads, long curly tails or natural
stubs.[16] Dog coats are sometimes wiry, other times smooth,
or even absent (there are a few hairless breeds). The genetic
diversity of *canis familiaris* is not only amazing and, as far
as humans are concerned, quite useful, but it also makes this
species a gold mine for researchers in genetics and for breed-
ers alike.[17]

Yet, some of the breeds humans have molded by selecting
for specific physical or behavioral traits are loaded with problems and are, in many ways, like Frankenstein's Creature.
They are created by humans and loved by a few, but they
are also plagued by genetic issues that affect their health and
well being. This has particularly been the case over the last
two hundred years, as humans have intentionally bred many
dogs for either aesthetic or behavioral traits, or sometimes

both, resulting in dogs who are ill equipped to live healthy and happy lives.

Australian terriers, Chesapeake Bay retrievers, greater Swiss mountain dogs, Portuguese water dogs, and Welsh springer spaniels are but a few of the dog breeds at elevated risk for epilepsy. English foxhounds, Rhodesian ridgebacks, Irish water spaniels, and Japanese chins, meanwhile, are much more likely to suffer from cancer. Heart disease, cataracts, autoimmune diseases, hip dysplasia—the list of potential genetic problems in dogs continues to grow.[18] It is interesting to note how many of these dogs are named for a specific location as well as for a particular task, thus pointing to a narrowing gene pool. Unaware of the inherent risks, humans produced dangerous genetic bottlenecks as dog breeds were fashioned.

The big, cute, bulging eyes of pugs and Boston terriers are certainly appealing. But when their eyes pop out of their heads, the genetic flaw is immediately apparent. Bred over generations for the aesthetic appeal of the big, baby-like eyes, the socket is now too shallow to hold the eye securely. Similarly, the squished-up nose of the bulldog is adorable, along with her funny snort; but it is much less charming when she is unable to breathe due to brachycephalic airway syndrome caused by the shortened snout. Dachshunds and basset hounds are humorous on their short legs with their long bodies, but the dwarfism bred into them over generations can lead to severe back problems. Just scratching the surface of genetic issues that were selected intentionally by humans reveals that the strength of the amazing dog genome—its variety and flexibility—can also be its weakness.

Angus was a double merle Australian shepherd—mostly white with haunting blue eyes. He was found stray and landed at a municipal animal shelter in Georgetown, Texas. His behavior there was erratic. Angus would bark wildly and lunge at the run when somebody approached. Eventually he was adopted, but the family returned him indicating that he was uncontrollable. This is not surprising to people who understand Australian shepherds (Aussies). The double merle, sometimes called "lethal white,"[19] is an example of breeding for aesthetics only, sometimes accidentally, and of creating a genetic bottleneck (figure 10).[20]

Aussies commonly have merle coloring, which basically means that their solid coat is broken up by patches of white or gray. Since the merle gene is dominant, if two merles are bred there is a strong likelihood that some of the puppies (based on genetic modeling it will be about one in four) will get merle genes from both parents. These puppies will have an almost solid white coat rather than the varied colors of a

Figure 10
Angus is a double merle (sometimes called "lethal white") Austra-
lian shepherd, a genetic combination that often results in vision and
hearing abnormalities. Photo courtesy of Dr. Jimmy Smith.

merle. What does this mean for those dogs? In many cases the double merle puppies develop hearing and vision problems. While the genetics are relatively complex, the outcomes are related to the lack of cells that produce pigment. The same genes that lead to a white coat also affect hair follicles in the ear passages and the development of the iris in the eye.[21] Interestingly for geneticists, certain other breeds of dogs who are not merle in color, but who can be white, have a higher occurrence of hearing problems—Dalmatians, boxers, and pit bulls are among those affected.

So why was the term "lethal white" applied to these double merle Aussies? While the outcome is sometimes loss of hearing and vision, these dogs can live long and healthy lives. But people are not always willing to maintain a dog who is different so, frequently, the white puppies were, and still are, killed—often, even before it is known if they are deaf or blind. For these puppies, their condition is lethal in the eyes of the humans who brought them into the world.

Angus made it out of the shelter, but not without a fight. The city decided that he was a danger to the public because of his vision and hearing problems, and they determined that he needed to be euthanized. A public outcry followed as word spread rapidly through social media that the old stigma of "lethal white" was being applied to Angus. Georgetown's city shelter Facebook page erupted with anger and even threats. A group of dog rescue volunteers finally convinced city officials to release him to a qualified rescue group. As a matter of fact, the city was eager to release him at that point in order to end the pressure that the outraged public was putting on city staff. Angus ended up catching his own personal flight from Texas to California, where he was placed with people who understood that double merle is not lethal, but rather that humans have made it so.

A celebrity dog has also become part of the purebred dog debate. Uga has been the name for the University of Georgia's mascot—a bulldog—for years. But when Uga VII died at the age of four in 2009 and Uga VIII died at the age of one and a half in 2011, even the fanatic mascot fans started to question the fitness of the breed. Bulldogs are, by most accounts, a genetic disaster. Their short nose, big eyes, and massive head lead to a variety of health problems, causing the average lifespan of these dogs to land at a very short six years. The "cuteness factor" of the bulldog has also led to its meteoric rise on the American Kennel Club's most popular breed list—going from number forty-one in 1973 to number six in 2010. To a certain extent, the appearance of the bulldog, and its popularity as a breed, could be related to the more humanlike qualities of a bulldog face.[22] Regardless, it is not a healthy look for a canine.

Genetic problems, however, are not the only outcome of the quest for purebred dogs. Another side effect of this increasing desire for specific breeds of dogs emerged after World War II in the United States—puppy mills. Because puppies were classified by the U.S. Department of Agriculture as an alternative crop for farmers, the regulations on breeding were minimal. Puppies became a commodity, and an attractive one at that. Rabbit hutches and chicken coops were repurposed for mass dog breeding. And there was a market for these mass produced, supposedly "purebred" dogs. As was the case in Victorian England, the rising middle class in the United States craved status symbols. Purebred dogs, rather than mixed breeds (mutts or curs), became fashionable. Pet stores popped up all over the United States, and in 1953 the popular song, "How Much Is That Doggie in the Window," held the number one spot on *Billboard* magazine's music chart for eight weeks.

Over the next fifty years puppy mills grew in scope and generally flew under the radar. Shopping malls had pet stores with puppies available for purchase (thus the doggie in the window song), and the public assumed all was well. Very few people who gazed into those shopping mall windows knew that puppy mills existed or that the cute puppies behind the glass were born in horrid conditions. One thing that never crossed the shoppers' minds was where these puppies had been before the store window, and where their parents were. When one digs more deeply, it becomes apparent quickly that these large-scale commercial operations are over-crowded and unsanitary. And that's a kind description. By the beginning of the twenty-first century there were between 2,000 and 3,000 licensed puppy producers in the country, along with an estimated 5,000–6,000 unlicensed.[23] Conditions in these facilities are horrid. Female breeding dogs are forced to have litters as frequently as possible; when they give birth, the puppies are held with them in a small pen without beds or human attention; and there is a very high mortality rate. But this is the system that must exist if dogs (puppies) become commodities—property to buy and sell. It is the antithesis of the dog-human relationship that has existed for millennia.

One unfortunate but unavoidable result of this process of mass production of puppies for sale is the reinforcement of practices that yield genetic-related health issues. As the smallest of the small Chihuahuas are bred together, the skull capacity continues to decrease and the dogs have no room for their brains. As the "merliest" of the merles are bred, beautiful puppies are born, but 25 percent of them have hearing or vision issues. To add to this genetic downside, the mass production facilities also lack early puppy care—nutritional deficiencies in their earliest weeks make for feeble and vulnerable puppies. The crowded conditions lead to the spread of disease. The puppies also lack socialization in the first eight weeks of their life, a significant window during which they should learn to interact not only with other dogs but with humans as well.

Over the last decade, information about puppy mills has started to reach the general public. Because of this, some businesses that operate as storefront retail establishments selling puppies have shut down. But the puppy mills continue, and sales through classified ads in local newspapers and, more significantly, over the Internet are exploding. "How much is that doggy in the window" has now become "how much is that doggy on the screen." These operations offer to ship puppies directly to the purchaser once they receive payment. With these various outlets for marketing and selling puppies, each year puppy mills generate between two and four million puppies that are then sold in the U.S.[24]

In response to the puppy mill tragedy, each of the last several sessions of the U.S. Congress has seen the introduction of the Puppy Uniform Protection and Safety Act (PUPS). The purpose of the act is to increase the welfare standards for dogs in high-volume breeding facilities. The minimal standards in the bill seem fairly easy to achieve. For example, dogs over twelve weeks of age need to be allowed to exercise once a day, enclosures must be cleaned once a day and be free of protruding objects. Yet even these basic levels of care are perceived as onerous by the puppy mill industry and, according to Congress' own information site, PUPS only has a 1 percent chance of passing.[25]

But the puppy mill industry and pet stores are not the only problem. Humans have bred very specific dogs for particular purposes for centuries. So, consider again the pit bull who, along with Staffordshire terriers and some other bully dog breeds, were bred, over generations, to bait bulls (thus the designation "bully breeds"). The crowds would watch a dog try to intimidate a bull, often by biting and holding onto the end of its nose. Eventually, primarily due to class politics (since this violent spectacle was aimed at the masses of impoverished people) and also to the growth of evangelical Christianity, with its condemnation of the gambling that went along with these fights, the brutal events were outlawed. One of the outcomes was decreasing demand for the bully breed dogs and, within twenty years, there were very few left.[26] Humans had created this dog over years for a specific purpose, then made their own creation, for all intents and purposes, illegal.

Different Sciences for Different Times?

"Yet you, my creator, detest and spurn me, thy creature, to whom thou art bound by ties only dissoluble by the annihilation of one of us. You purpose to kill me. How dare you sport thus with life? Do your duty towards me, and I will do mine towards the rest of mankind."

—*The Creature addressing Frankenstein*[27]

As the science of the eighteenth and nineteenth centuries played a major role in Shelley's tale of Frankenstein and his Creature (attempting to bring corpses to life with electricity), so does the science of the twenty-first century play a major role in discussions about dog breeds, including that elusive category of pit bulls. Since this group of dogs is not even an official breed, how does one decide if a dog is a pit bull? Official, related breeds are the Staffordshire bull terrier, American bulldog, boxer, and a few more. But the dog still cannot be certified since he or she has an undetermined breed.[28]

Because the range of morphology is as wide as the genealogical record, new ways to determine which dogs are pit bulls and which are not are becoming increasingly commonplace. For example, many owners send off swabs from the cheeks of their canine companions to laboratories for DNA tests. Examples abound of dogs who look like pit bulls but turn out to be combinations of everything from poodles to Irish wolfhounds to golden retrievers. Numerous compilations of images show a variety of dogs, many appearing to bear the physical characteristics of pit bulls, accompanied by a few looking like anything but a pit bull.[29] Of course, those few who look nothing like pit bulls are the ones who turn out to have pit bull DNA, while the large-headed and -mouthed stocky dogs are, usually, as much golden retriever or other seemingly benign type of dog as any other breed. It is a strange exercise of science in the early twenty-first century, that as long as your DNA clears you, you are clear of the offending label.

Culture is in conflict regarding pit bulls, along with some other breeds. The stereotype of a "breed" that is not even a recognized breed can be undermined, indeed disproved, by the most revered of contemporary scientific knowledge—the proof of DNA. But even DNA evidence is not sufficient, in too many cases, to save this creature from its modern-day angry mob. Breed Specific Legislation (BSL) bans pit bulls (and pit bull–like dogs) from rental properties, neighborhoods, and even entire cities or counties, indeed possibly even states.[30] The most widely publicized breed specific bans in the U.S. are in Denver, Colorado, and Miami-Dade County, Florida. There are also bans on bully breeds that cover large portions of Canada and Australia, and the U.K. (the country where they were first "created").

But on the very local level, breed bans have the greatest impact. The most affordable rental properties often ban bully breed dogs, putting their owners, who often have few other options, into situations where they must surrender their dog to the local animal control agency. Because of this, municipal animal shelters are frequently bursting at the seams with pit bull type dogs; over one third of all dogs at shelters are pit bulls.[31] Even with advocacy groups working to educate the public on pit bulls, the euthanasia rates for these homeless dogs remain astonishingly high, with over 1 million pit bulls killed in the U.S. every year.

Part of the reasoning behind such bans is based on dog-bite data. On the surface, it appears that certain types of dogs—pit bulls and Rottweilers specifically—are involved in dog-bite incidents more frequently than other types of dog. But even the Centers for Disease Control, which collects this data, points out that it is faulty and unreliable for several reasons. One of the primary reasons is the difficulty of even collecting data that is accurate. A dog's breed can be mis-labeled, bites can go unreported, and multiple factors can contribute to incidents. In the long run, dynamics other than breed are better indicators of whether or not a dog is more likely to bite. If dogs are chained or tethered, or if they are unaltered (not neutered), the bite rate is much higher, regardless of breed.[32]

As the National Canine Research Council carefully concludes in its response to dog-bite research, the model for determining the cause of dog bites, which is based on traditional public health analysis of a disease, is not appropriate. The factors leading to a dog bite are so complex that they cannot be attributed to any one cause. Indeed, as these researchers claim, single-cause explanations, primarily focused on blaming a specific breed of dog, have "hindered scientific inquiry and prevented the development of better informed public policy."[33] Attempting to isolate these dog-specific factors without taking into account the entire situation, particularly the actions of the humans involved, leads to inaccurate and even dangerously unsubstantiated conclusions. The one factor that is a reliable predictor, and there has been consensus on this for over fifty years, is the behavior of humans.[34]

But pit bulls still bear the brunt of the dog-bite mania that, all too often, leads to a monster hunt. For the first half of the twentieth century, pit bulls were media darlings. As we saw, Sergeant Stubby (c. 1916–1926) was the most decorated war dog in World War I. Pit bulls graced the covers of popular magazines including *Life* and *Parade*.[35] They were portrayed as American heroes and even as wounded war veterans. Dogs such as Petey, of "Little Rascals" fame, and Tige, from the Buster Brown Shoe advertisements, were viewed as symbols of loyalty, bravery, and safety (figure 11).

By the end of the twentieth century though, pit bulls were connected with dog fighting and, just as their bully breed ancestors in the nineteenth century were labeled as unsavory in Britain, so were they.[36] The sensational case of Michael Vick, the professional football player, and his fighting-dog ring hit the media with fury.[37] In 2007 investigators raided property owned by Vick in southern Virginia and found over seventy dogs there—mostly pit bulls. They had been used as

Figure 11
Phoebe was surrendered to a municipal shelter because of breed restrictions put in place by a landlord. Later, she was returned to her family and certified as a service dog for their disabled child.
Photo courtesy of Dr. Jimmy Smith.

part of a fighting ring. Some of the dogs required humane euthanasia immediately, others went to be rehabilitated. Twenty-two of the dogs were relocated to Best Friends Animal Sanctuary in Utah. While some of these were adopted to new, safe homes under the "Vicktory" dogs program, a final tragedy (not widely reported) still hit the Vick fighting dogs— babesia gibsoni, a fatal disease.[38] This parasite is spread by blood-to-blood contact, which means it is frequently found in dogs used for fighting, and it eventually destroys red blood cells and causes premature death. Even though some of Vick's dogs survived the fighting rings, many will still die as a result of human negligence and cruelty.[39]

Breeding, marketing, mass production, fighting, genetic bottlenecks—all of these are aspects of the modern story of dogs of design in the United States, Europe and, increasingly, on an almost global scale. A fraught history of selective breeding has led to dogs who are unhealthy and short-lived. An equally fraught history of abuse and of misconceptions about certain breeds leaves a trail of tragic, untimely death at the direct hands of humans. Breed stigmas impact both dogs, particularly pit bulls, and the people who live with those dogs. These unsubstantiated labels lead to modern-day witch hunts and reinforce prejudices such that many dogs who were once seen as heroes are now viewed as monsters and outlaws.[40]

Chapter 6

- - - - - - - - - -

The Dog-Human Bond
Domesticating Each Other

*Our animal companions awaken within us a capacity for
love that I believe cannot be derived elsewhere. In just
eight brief months, our beloved Tillie birthed within me
an ability to bravely care, nurture and love & I will be
forever grateful for this gentle, soulful, sweet beauty. She
died early this morning during a seizure that would not let
go. I am blessed to have been with her and pray that she
knew she was not alone.*

—*Christine K*[1]

The lead article of the Sunday, February 17, 2013, *Austin
American-Statesman*,[2] occupying the top two-thirds of the
"Life" section of the newspaper, was "Welcome to Dogtown:
We love our canine friends—and we're not alone in making
dogs part of the family." The headline image accompany-
ing the article was a picture of a bride with her 10-year-old
Australian shepherd mix; the caption explained that her dog
"served as one of the six bridesmaids in the wedding party."
Other stories in this newspiece described a woman who does
yoga with her schnauzer-poodle mix (Stella), a Great Dane

romp at one of Austin's off-leash dog parks, a report on taking dogs to work (including a picture of an art director at an
advertising firm working on a project with his dachshund in
his lap), and listings of the many pet-friendly condominiums
and restaurants in the city.

The statistics reported by the Sunday newspaper in central Texas that morning reveal what might be interpreted as a
significant cultural shift. For example, Austin has 365 veterinarians, not far behind the estimated 400–450 pediatricians,
practicing in the city. There is a rapidly growing market for
doggy daycare, professional establishments that provide all
of the dog's needs while the human is at work or elsewhere.
This service, comparable to that for child daycare, offers an
additional insight into the changing role of dogs in this trendy,
modern city—and many similar cities around the world. Both
the growing number of veterinarians and the increasing avail-
ability of doggy daycare suggest an equivalency, or at least
something of a comparison, between the prevalence of services for dogs and children. The fact that in 2013 an estimated
7.2 million dogs live in Texas, more than in any other state in
the U.S., was also emphasized in the article—and this statistic
was proclaimed with a significant amount of pride, as is often
the case in Texas.[3] But, even more interestingly, the report suggested in not-so-subtle terms that the role of dogs is changing dramatically and even essentially. Dogs are, according to
this view, becoming something different than they have ever
been in the past. Their very being in relationship to humans
is venturing into unexplored territory.[4] Asking why these
assumptions of the morphing human-dog relationship perme-
ate popular culture and imagination is an important question.
It ponders ongoing issues of humans' always shifting ideas
about themselves as well as their practical doings.

Indeed, changes to the place of the dog in contemporary culture need to be taken seriously and considered both

thoughtfully and in distinct contexts globally. In some societies the dog-human relationship is different than it has been in centuries past, but it is also the same in intriguing and illuminating ways. There are a variety of reasons offered by those who suggest that the relationship of dogs and humans has changed drastically, though some of these seem questionable. Dogs are filling a role of deep companionship in some arguably new ways. But when one reviews the entire history of the human-dog partnership, dogs always have been companions. Today, dogs are service animals and comforters, but so were dogs in the ancient world. In the twenty-first century, dogs are being incorporated into religious ideas and practices, but that also is one of the markers of the earliest human-dog interaction. Increasingly dogs are front and center in reports from the battlefield, but they were already there when the pharaohs waged their wars over four millennia ago.

So in ways that are sometimes hiding in plain sight and at other times mirroring the past, dogs are in general still in the same relationship with humans as they have been for thousands of years. Amazingly, dogs have always been there, walking right next to humans, sitting under their tables, curling up next to them at night to sleep, helping humans fight for food and struggle for survival, posing the question of what it means to be human, and what it means to be dog. While some people argue that dogs are entering a new gray area that they have not inhabited before, these canines have been in gray areas for thousands of years. In this ability to shift roles and fill new spaces in the human orbit, they are a unique, fascinating, even symbiotic, example of a species with whom humans walk the planet.

Even with that stated, dogs are morphing, just as humans are—changing together as these two species have for 30,000 years. Humans and dogs have traveled a winding and changing road together for millennia. At various intersections new challenges confronted both species, but the partnership did not wane. In all of their incarnations, maybe each is not human or dog without the other. The role of the dog-human relationship is not dramatically changing; it is continuing to adapt as it always has.

While dogs are taking on some modified roles, they are definitely not entirely new characters in the ongoing human-dog drama, but rather just amplified or reconsidered players. In other words, the dog-human relationship is an ancient and persistent one. It is not novel, though reactions to it are coming from novel settings (such as the multibillion dollar pet food and product industry, as well as current technologies that provide dogs with the possibility of having their own Facebook pages—or, more to the point, for a human to create one for them). And, for interesting cultural reasons, these morphing roles for dogs show up on the radar screen for news organizations and researchers, where they are made into something novel and thus seem like a new experience in human history. Yet, it is not a new phenomenon for people to find food for dogs, or for dogs to accompany humans on every daily venture. The normative relationship for dogs and humans is constant companionship—eating together, walking side-by-side, hunting together, sleeping next to each other, fighting together, pondering eternity with each other, or at least the human is considering the dog's coeternity. But the status of dogs and their overarching roles have not changed as much as some might suggest.[5] The human-dog bond was initiated as long ago as 30,000 years, and it has been solid, and in many ways consistent, ever since.

As various theories arise to suggest that something radical is happening, humans owe it to dogs to recognize and reclaim the history of their longest-standing partner. Not doing so diminishes the bond that the two species have built through countless generations. But not claiming this history also threatens to skew the relationship, to put the burden on dogs to find a way to fit in, or else. And by not recognizing this mutual affiliation, humans deny their own responsibility to continue to live side-by-side with dogs.

One of the reasons this recognition and remembering are imperative speaks to a central reality of the dog-human journey—it has, at its core, a religious connection. Which also means that the canine-human story has the questions of who humans think they are in the world, and of what truly matters to them. Denying the role of dogs not only diminishes dogs, it diminishes humanity. Humans are essentially connected to other species; they cannot live without intimate companionship with others. It makes humans human. Dogs reveal this wonderful reality more deeply than any other species.

Canine Religiosus?

Run on the right path, past the two brindled,
four-eyed dogs . . .
guardian dogs, the four-eyed keepers of the path,
who watch over men.

—*Rig Veda*, 10.12.10–10.14.10[6]

Not only were dogs pragmatic partners for thousands of years, dogs were also spiritual companions following a parallel and intertwined path with humans. Throughout these thirty millennia, dogs assisted in the hunt and the herd, served as healers, accompanied humans in the journey to the afterlife, served as tools of war and empire, provided deep companionship and, unintentionally, helped to decimate many other species. But they were also avatars of divinities and actors in a variety of myths and legends. They were central players in religious stories and practices. The relationship is both more and less religious, or maybe just religious in a different way, as humans and dogs enter the twenty-first century together. Maybe dogs are not official guides to the afterlife as they were in the Greek world or in the Vedic tradition, but humans are incorporating them into rituals of remembrance, and hoping for a canine presence in eternity, just as they have for thousands of years.

A quick glance through the website "dog-church.com" provides a glimpse into the new ways that dogs act as spiritual companions in an ever-changing religious landscape. The creator of this site owns and operates a dog boarding facility and daycare. But Sunday is the day when other staff members are off, so she is alone with the dogs. This is when she realizes something deep and spiritual happening in her relationship with canines:

> It is my time to reflect, worship, forgive and give thanks for all that I have been blessed with. Dogs are amazing teachers if we take the time to observe and listen with more than our eyes and ears. When we spend time with dogs, we learn how to listen with our hearts and to see life in a new and very different way. When I finish a hike with the dogs my soul is rejuvenated and my spirit is set free. The experience is like church . . . like Dog-Church.[7]

The musings on dog-church are just one of the many ways that the virtual world is reaffirming, albeit in a new medium, the deep connections between humans and dogs.

But dogs are also being invited into other, more traditional worship spaces again—and not only as part of rituals of death and bereavement (though those are indeed quite significant). On a Saturday in New Jersey at a traditional havdalah service, a Jewish ritual welcoming the new week, worshipers gathered in a rather nontraditional spot, the parking lot. This was the fifth annual pet blessing at the synagogue, and dogs were happily bounding around the worshipers.[8] Jewish blessings of pets take place annually from California to Texas to

Pennsylvania to New Jersey, usually during the fall when the portion of the Torah focusing on the story of Noah is read. And dogs are the main attendees, as they are in Christian, Interfaith, Buddhist, and Wiccan blessing services (just to name a few) around the world.

Since the 1970s the practice of blessing animals has reemerged in religious communities after going somewhat dormant for generations.[9] In many of these settings, dogs are the primary companions in attendance. The reasons are practical, but they also speak to their special relationship. While other companion animals are also undeniably important, dogs are the ones who naturally accompany humans into the various settings of human culture. Because they have journeyed next to humans for thousands of years, they are (mostly) comfortable in the midst of crowds and even enjoy going with humans. Watching a dog bound into a car, the new way of "going with," speaks to the ease with which the two species move around together. Thus, into the worship arena they go.[10]

An additional avenue of connection through traditional religious communities is providing veterinary care for animals. In an interesting bookend to the participation of dogs in the cultic healing rituals of ancient cultures, religious communities are providing modern health care for dogs whose people are unable to afford these necessary services. Just following the turn of the twenty-first century, the Humane Society of the United States established a faith-based outreach program. They keep track of some of the special outreach programs provided throughout the U.S. One effort, sponsored by and held at Church of the King outside of New Orleans, offers monthly veterinary services for people in the community. The lines stretch around the block, with hundreds of people and their pets waiting patiently for the much-needed medical care.[11] Other groups, like St. Martin's Animal Foundation in

Los Angeles, directly connect their work in dog rescue to a
religious calling.[12]

While dogs are reentering the sanctuary spaces, outreach
ministries, and mortuary rituals of various religious traditions worldwide, these are not the only ways that dogs continue to serve as spiritual companions. An entirely new world
of religious meaning is growing out of dog rescue culture,
particularly in the U.S., Canada, and western Europe, but
increasingly on a global scale. In this world of meaning making, the question, with certain religious underpinnings, frequently posed is "Who Rescued Who?"[13]

"Who Rescued Whom?"

My life alone, abandoned, scared.
Eyes pleading, heart willing, soul bared.
I have hope. Ready, willing, loving, open, strong.
Won't you notice me, see me, find me, bring me along?
There she is, I think, the one who will look this way,
see me.
I stand up straight, look brave, must wag and smile,
please see me.
She's turning, kneeling, thinking, watching, reaching,
loving. It's me she's taking!
Together we are saved, she took me, I wag, lick her.
My heart and my body—no longer breaking.[14]

It is amazing to see how many bumper stickers and window magnets reading "Who Rescued Who?" adorn cars in
the U.S.[15] These public placards raise a powerful question,
as well as a statement of solidarity. For generations dogs
have been a natural, taken-for-granted part of human culture, unquestioned in terms of their presence. But as human
culture became increasingly technologized and sanitized, the
place of dogs was questioned and regulated. For most of
human and dog history, the dog was a constant, unassuming,

and unquestioned presence. Dogs were just there, wherever "there" might be—a field, a ship, a barn, a house, a battleground. But after the Enlightenment, with the rise of ideas and practices that emphasized human superiority and centrality (anthropocentrism), the significant presence of any other animal threatened the assumed superior place of humans. Even dogs, who were the central and irreplaceable partners and companions in human endeavors, needed to be categorized as property—as "things" rather than as sentient, living beings.[16] Any animal other than the human, who was no longer considered to be an animal but as something other and superior, was denigrated and discarded. As the seminal Enlightenment period philosopher René Descartes claimed, animals, most certainly including dogs, are mere machines, whereas humans have souls and are capable of thought.[17]

Eventually, both cultural and scientific insights challenged those assumptions and presumptions. But cultural practices take decades, and maybe even centuries, to reform. Globally, the control of dog populations assumes that dogs are expendable, unimportant to human culture. Thousands of dogs are killed by humans every day because they are considered unnecessary or, more directly, a mere nuisance. This happens for a variety of reasons, all culturally variable. In some places, dogs are still viewed as pariahs—as pests who are not fully integrated into human culture—even though they are nothing if not a domesticated species. This is the dilemma of being a dog! Dogs only exist as a domesticated species, they live in relationship and rely on that connection with humans. But they are still placed into the category of pest or pariah by many humans, thus threatening their survival.

In response to this denial of the significance of dogs, among other animals, and of their perilous situation in human society, some people choose to spend their time and energy engaged in rescue efforts. From local shelters to specific breed

rescue groups to national and international relocation of
homeless dogs, rescue takes myriad forms. But in almost all
cases, rescue responds to the basic, and sometime startling,
facts of the situation. In the U.S. alone, for example, approximately two million dogs are surrendered to shelters annually and 60 percent of these are euthanized because there are
no humans who will take responsibility for them.[18] Rescue
groups try to fill this gap.

The scale of these efforts became apparent with the news
coverage following Hurricane Katrina. As the storm hit New
Orleans and the surrounding areas, images of stranded people were stark and horrifying. It was clear that the response
to the disaster was utterly inadequate; the devastation and
human suffering were shocking. But then a second story,
and one that cannot be totally disconnected from that of
human suffering, came to the surface. Companion animals,
both dogs and cats, were left behind. Estimates range from
50,000 to over 200,000 pets who were stranded, many alone
for weeks and even months, following the storm. And many
humans, in a quest to save their dogs, also stayed behind to
weather the hurricane. In the days that followed, people from
all over the U.S. headed in the direction of New Orleans to
try to rescue the animals.[19] While some cats were rescued,
they are simply much harder to find. But many dogs, as is
their nature, continued to look for humans to help get them
out of the battered city. The rescue efforts changed the face of
disaster planning forever and shed new light on the continuing significance of dogs in human culture. In the end, over
10,000 animals, mostly dogs, were rescued from the city. Stories of bravery and compassion, as well as stories of brutality
and indifference, rose to the surface after the flood.

While the relationship between humans and dogs has
remained in many ways the same, dogs have become increasingly vulnerable in a world where they are primarily pets

whose well-being is frequently at the whim of their human companions.[20] Because of this, more and more humans understand their role as rescuers, though even in the midst of that they self-identify as having been rescued by dogs. In the documentary *Dark Water Rising: Survival Stories of Hurricane Katrina Animal Rescue*, the lives of the human activists involved in post-Katrina rescue reveal the depth of meaning apparent in their efforts. Images of people risking their own lives, combing through the wreckage, trying not to inhale black mold or slice their bodies open climbing through windows, suggests a commitment worth dying for. Several of the rescuers lost everything they had before the efforts—family, jobs, homes—in order to save the dogs.

And dog rescuers come in all shapes and sizes, from various backgrounds and income levels. Emmylou Harris, a popular country music star, established Bonaparte's Retreat, a dog rescue sanctuary, in her own backyard in Nashville. She claims,

> One of the great things about dogs, they are totally in the moment, and I think that's a very difficult thing for humans to do. We're cursed with self-consciousness. We can't get away from ourselves. You asked me if I have any regrets? I regret that it took me all that time to figure out I could have a dog on the road.[21]

Harris directly connects finding meaning in her rescue efforts with dogs, and employs overtly religious language to do so.

Whether rescue and activist work with dogs is identified as "quasi-religious" by those involved, or as a more direct salvation-type experience,[22] it certainly fits easily with the definition of religion as committing life to what matters the most[23]—in this case, what matters to many of those involved in rescue is the human-dog bond.[24] Rescuers fly across continents, stay awake night after night, put dogs before family and friends, and more. In interviews conducted with dog rescuers, statements of commitment included: "I would run out on the interstate to save a dog"; "My last marriage ended because of foster dogs"; "I would drive to the end of the world to save a dog."[25] While some of these claims might seem extreme, they speak to the religious nature of the obligation dog rescuers feel for the dogs.

Randy Grim, a dog rescuer in Saint Louis, touchingly believes that the dogs who run the streets of the city call to him, saying, "don't leave me here."[26] Grim spends most of his income—interestingly, earned as a dog groomer for wealthy

Figure 12
These puppies were orphaned when they were two days old, so all were bottle-fed by human foster parents. Puppies' eyes and ears are closed until they are 10–14 days old, so they survive by scent. Bottle puppies gravitate to hands of their fosterers as they would to their mother, and nurse on fingers. These particular puppies were fostered by the author. Photo courtesy of Dr. Jimmy Smith.

dog owners—and all of his spare time finding homeless dogs and rehoming them. His connection to dogs has, in his mind, saved his life—or, rather, given him a life. Maybe this is because of the history humans share with dogs. Humans are who we are in large part because dogs have shared this life with us.

The Two Ends of the Leash . . .

Amazingly, dogs continue in a wide variety of roles—as hunters and herders, as healers and warriors, as invaders and companions—even when technologies and cultures change drastically. Granted they are also "pets" (companions) on a scale never before experienced in human-dog culture, but even the idea of the pet is one that is constantly argued and changing.[27] While the role of pet is a somewhat exaggerated, and sometimes problematic, one for dogs to fill in some settings, it is not a novel reality. Still, and mostly in response to the pet phenomenon, people are rethinking how to live with and provide for dogs who are abandoned or mistreated, as well as pampered pooches. Dog rescue efforts become central to the lives of scores of humans, and dogs fill the place of children in some family structures. The "new work of dogs" is quite complicated to say the least, even though it is not entirely new at all.

Notes

Introduction

1   The author in no way buys into the myth of progress. These changes are not necessarily positive trajectories—they are, rather, different ways of being.

Chapter 1

1   Lorenz, *King Solomon's Ring*, 29. This book is one of the major works by the twentieth-century Austrian ethologist and Nobel prize–winner Konrad Lorenz. He deals specifically with the role of dogs in the chapter "The Covenant." Lorenz also wrote a book in 2002 dedicated almost completely to the human-dog relationship, *Man Meets Dog*. In this book he compares the relationship between humans and cats with that between humans and dogs.

2   The language used from this point forward is proto-dog, the dog before the dog or the ancestor of the dog linking the wolf and the dog. There is general archaeological consensus that the canine in Chauvet Cave is not a domesticated dog, but rather an in-between dog and wolf canine.

3   For purposes of dating, I will reference "years ago" or "BP" (before present). Archaeologists have been using radiocarbon dating for over sixty years and reference the "present" as 1950 (the date when this technology was developed). There are adjustments made to this dating technique, so in archaeological research the designations used are "BP" (before present) and "cal BP" (calibrated years before present). The "cal BP" designation takes into account scientifically based adjustments to

the years before present. I make every attempt to use the "cal BP" years throughout for consistency's sake, but am using BP in the text for ease of reading.

4   Scholars obviously cannot claim with complete certainty that these footprints were made at the exact same time, but their proximity in the fossilized mud is convincing and the image of a child and dog walking through the darkness together evokes an early bond. For information on dating of the footprints, see Harrington, "Human Footprints."

5   Clottes, "Chauvet Cave." Found online at http://www.metmuseum.org/ toah/hd/chav/hd_chav.htm (accessed May 4, 2013).

6   For more information on Chauvet Cave, go to the French Cultural Ministry's website at http://www.culture.gouv.fr/culture/arcnat/chauvet/en/ (accessed May 4, 2013).

7   For information on research concluding that dogs existed over 100,000 years ago, see the mitochondrial DNA studies conducted by Vila, Maldonado, and Wayne, "Phylogenetic Relationships." For information on research concluding that dogs existed at least 26,000 years ago, see Germonpré et al., "Fossil Dogs"; Germonpré, Lázničková-Galetová, and Sablin, "Palaeolithic Dog Skulls"; and Ovodov et al., "A 33,000-Year-Old Incipient Dog"; among other studies.

8   Zooarchaeology is a relatively new field. Before the 1970s, very few archaeologists focused on relationships between humans and other animals. For more information on this history, see N. Russell, *Social Zooarchaeology*.

9   Sufficient evidence and numerous publications advance the well-accepted theory that wolves are the direct ancestors of dogs, so I will not elaborate on that claim here. For more information, see Morey, *Dogs: Domestication*; Wayne, "Molecular Evolution"; Wozencraft, "Carnivora: Canidae"; and Coppinger and Coppinger, *Dogs: A Startling New Understanding*.

10   As Larson et al. state clearly in their recently published research: "despite the volume of new data, estimates of when, where, and how many times dogs were domesticated remain disconcertingly imprecise" ("Rethinking Dog Domestication," 2).

11   Jared Diamond makes this point in his overview of world history, *Guns, Germs and Steel*, 37. Most likely, zooarchaeologists, behaviorists, and environmental historians will continue to debate the question of the first dog for years to come. In this major work, however, Diamond does not address dogs at much length, he focuses on other, agriculture-related animals such as cattle and sheep. This is one area, in my opinion, that is lacking in Diamond's otherwise admirable, wide-ranging study.

12   See Savolainen et al., "Genetic Evidence," for a study concluding that all dogs come from East Asian canine populations.

13   Pionnier-Capitan et al., "New Evidence," 2123.

14   See Vigne, "L'humérus de chien"; Pionnier-Capitan et al., "New Evidence"; Benecke, "Studies on Early Dog Remains."

15 The definition of "species" is itself an evolving one. The most commonly held definition, as emphasized by Clutton-Brock, *Natural History*, is "a species is a group of interbreeding natural populations that is genetically isolated from other such groups as a result of physiological or behavioural barriers"; whereas the "commonly held view that the separation of two species can be determined by whether or not they will produce fertile offspring when interbred . . . is a quite inadequate means of defining a species" (4)—a view endorsed by many biologists and zoologists (and zooarchaeologists).

16 Early humans likely mastered the use of fire by at least 250,000 years ago and, as they emerged from Africa, carried this important skill with them. Other animals are also known to use fire to a certain extent, carefully foraging to eat nuts and other food items after forest or brush fires have, essentially, cooked them. This may have been the way that humans also discovered the important use of fire as a tool in preparing food.

17 Germonpré et al., "Fossil Dogs," 474.

18 Germonpré et al., "Fossil Dogs," 489.

19 As Germonpré and her team note, "it is likely that a number of Palaeolithic dog remains have so far not been recognized" ("Fossil Dogs," 473).

20 See Ovodov et al., "A 33,000-Year-Old Incipient Dog," for comments on the analyses provided by Germonpré et al., suggesting that these earliest remains do not indicate a "putative Palaeolithic" dog, but rather a wolf expressing morphological characteristics influenced by sharing ecological niches with humans, and that more research does need to be conducted before definite claims can be forwarded regarding the existence of dogs before the Last Glacial Maximum.

21 Not all archaeologists agree that the proto-dogs were actually a distinct species from wolves. Whether and when dogs formed distinct populations, not different species, remains in question.

22 See Benecke, "Studies on Early Dog Remains."

23 The definition of evolution widely accepted by biologists is "changes in the genetic makeup of populations of organisms over generations." Thus evolution occurs "across all scales, from individual populations to species and on up to kingdoms." See E. Russell, *Evolutionary History*, chap. 1.

24 Scholars frequently point out that remains of dogs easily pass unnoticed. For example, in their work on "Early Archaic Domestic Dogs," in Crockford, *Dogs Through Time*, Yohe and Pavesic state that although "the postcranial specimens were recognized as canid during the analysis of the human skeletal material, the skulls had been misplaced and did not resurface for several years" (94). See also Warren, "Palaeopathology of Archaic Period Dogs," in Crockford, *Dogs Through Time*: "Despite their numbers, the dogs buried at Archaic sites in the Southeast have been largely ignored by archaeozoologists, and their use and treatment in life remains a subject of speculation" (105).

25 Combining genetic and archaeological research, Raisor, *Determining the Antiquity of Dog Origins*, develops a compelling thesis in her dissertation. She suggests that "natural evolutionary divergence occurred without human intervention" (247), which is a version of what is proposed in this chapter as well.

26 The debate about Neanderthals continues to evolve. Some studies suggest that *Homo sapiens* and Neanderthals intermixed, other studies conclude that the traces of Neanderthal DNA in some Europeans derive from an ancestor they shared with *Homo sapiens*. Regardless, following the Last Glacial Maximum, Neanderthals, as a distinct existing hominid species, were no longer found in Eurasia.

27 Raymond and Lorna Coppinger, dog behaviorists and researchers, focus on this particular trait—"flight distance"—as the basis for the self-domestication of dogs: "The wild wolf, *canis lupus*, began to separate into populations that could make a living at the dumps and those that couldn't. Within one segment of the population, the frequency increased of those genes that resulted in tamer wolves, and that population could be said to have been evolving toward a new species." Coppinger and Coppinger, *Dogs*, 61.

28 See the farm fox experiment (Trut, "Early Canid Domestication") for more information on this domestication process and how it has been accomplished in other canine species in a controlled setting.

29 E. Russell points to the "odds of survival for tamer animals" when they "killed off the hellions among the wolves lurking about camp" (*Evolutionary History*, 81). Russell makes a strong argument for the unintentional impact of humans on the evolution of other species. By changing the local environment (e.g., rapidly depleting a particular resource or selecting for certain animals without realizing why they were doing so), humans impacted the evolution of a number of other species. This process of unintentional impact on the evolution of other species is not exclusive to humans—other species have done the same. E.g., Michael Pollan in *The Botany of Desire* makes the argument that bees have significantly impacted the evolution of numerous flower-bearing plants (8–9).

30 Crockford, "Dog Evolution: A Role," in Crockford, *Dogs Through Time*, 12–13.

31 Crockford, "Dog Evolution: A Role," in Crockford, *Dogs Through Time*, 12–13.

32 Clutton-Brock and Kitchener, "An Anomalous Wolf," in Crockford, *Dogs Through Time*, 264. These authors suggest that hybridization is quite harmful in the contemporary period when wild wolf populations are threatened globally. Governmental authorities rarely recognize the hybridized animals as endangered, and their morphology can negatively affect the survival possibilities of hybrids in the wild.

33 See Pennisi,"Diet Shaped Dog Domestication," n.p.

34 See Pappas, "Starchy Diets." In the article, Erik Axelsson, one of the

lead researchers on the team, who discovered this parallel genetic development, observed, "it's cool that we've shared an environment for such a long time and we've eaten the same kind of food for such a long time, that we have started to become more similar in that way," n.p.

35 By this stage *Homo erectus* and other early humans had experienced a series of major diet shifts. They had gone from eating primarily foods they could gather (nuts, fruits, roots) to combining that with foods they could hunt (animal flesh) to cooking some of these foods and making them more easily digestible. At the time humans and dogs were pairing up, they were adding more starchy foods to these diets, the penultimate step to major agricultural production of corn, wheat, rice, potatoes, and soy—staples of the human diet for the last several thousand years.

36 Crockford, "Dog Evolution: A Role," in Crockford, *Dogs Through Time*, 12.

37 At least this is the case as of the time this book was written. Zooarchaeological evidence is changing constantly, and there will most likely be a different—and earlier—dog who is the first accepted dog.

38 Larson et al., "Rethinking Dog Domestication," 1.

39 Jared Diamond points this out in *Guns, Germs and Steel*, stating that only 14 domesticated large mammals out of 148 "candidates" for domestication actually became domesticated. In this far-ranging study, Diamond makes a strong argument for how this process occurred. As mentioned in the note above, however, there is one major omission from his study of the process of domestication: dogs. Not only is their impact on the process not mentioned, but neither is the fact that although wolves do not have the shared characteristics that would make them a candidate for domestication, nevertheless dogs are the first domesticated animal.

40 See Trut, "Early Canid Domestication"; Morey, *Dogs: Domestication*.

41 Trut, "Early Canid Domestication," 163.

42 Studies indicate that these changes were centered in the thyroid. Susan Crockford, "Dog Evolution" (2008), suggests that thyroxine production is affected by adaptation to stress.

43 See Crockford, "Dog Evolution: A Role," in Crockford, *Dogs Through Time*, 11–14.

44 Crockford and others contend that this variability in dogs is rooted in the hybridization of dogs and wolves that occurred over millennia: "the unique situation resulting from the early prehistoric expansion of the dog (*canis familiaris*) into territories occupied by its ancestral species, the grey wolf (*canis lupus*). The extraordinary extent of sympatric distribution of dog and wolf is an unprecedented situation among domesticates, resulting in a myriad of potential hybrid zones that have existed for thousands of years. Indeed both morphological and genetic evidence suggest that occasional hybridization must have occurred between these two species and that wolves may have been more affected genetically by these events than dogs" (Crockford, "Commentary on Dog Evolution,"

in Crockford, *Dogs Through Time*, 295). See also, "This result suggests that either wolves were domesticated in several places and at different times or that there was one domestication event followed by several episodes of admixture between dogs and wolves. Whichever is the case, the results imply that dogs have a diverse origin involving more than one wolf population" (Vila, Maldonado, and Wayne, "Phylogenetic Relationships," 73).

45 Valensi, "Archaeozoology of Lazaret Cave," 361.

46 Clutton-Brock, *Natural History*, 3.

47 Derr, *Dog's Best Friend*, 19. Here Derr claims that it "is more likely that throughout the Northern Hemisphere these precursors of modern humans and wolves lived and hunted in close proximity than that these three sites represent an accidental accumulation of old bones."

48 Sablin and Khlopachev, "Earliest Ice Age Dogs," 798. The researchers concluded that these early dogs "may have played an important role in the development of human hunting technology and strategy."

49 See Musil, "Evidence for Domestication of Wolves," in Crockford, *Dogs Through Time*, 25.

50 Musil, "Evidence for Domestication of Wolves," in Crockford, *Dogs Through Time*, 26. In his fascinating research on this topic, Rudolf Musil comes to the conclusion that "the first domestication of wolves may be thus connected with the hunting of horses."

51 There is still dispute about when and how this migration happened, some arguing for as long as 30,000 years ago, with migrations across the ocean from Polynesia and Australia, while others argue for a later migration from northeast Asia. I will follow archaeological evidence here, which indicates that the first humans inhabited the Americas approximately 12,000 years ago.

52 Saunders and Daeschler, "Descriptive Analyses," 21–23.

53 Fiegel, "Healing Power of Dogs," 13.

54 See Diamond, *Guns, Germs and Steel*; E. Russell, *Evolutionary History*; and Stanford, "Bison Kill by Ice Age Hunters." This is a fairly contested theory. Many scholars argue that the anthropogenic extinction theory for megafauna on all continents except Africa is not valid, but rather climate change was the main cause of these extinctions. Still, humans and dogs have been the cause of species extinction in the modern period, an issue discussed in a later chapter.

55 See Shigehara and Hongo, "Ancient Remains of Jomon Dogs," in Crockford, *Dogs Through Time*.

56 Tintararat, Wadi Teshuinat, Tadrart Acacus, Libyan Sahara. An image of this painting can be found at http://www.flickr.com/photos/82822788@N00/442278366 (accessed August 17, 2012).

57 Object held at the Metropolitan Museum of Art, New York. Accession no. 40.2.1.

58 Manaserian and Antonian, "Dogs of Armenia," in Crockford, *Dogs Through Time*, 220.

59 Gatto, "Aswan Area," 12–14.

60 Olsen, "Secular and Sacred Roles": "The close association of dogs and horses may also reflect the use of dogs in hunting, or perhaps horse herding" (90).

61 See Diamond, *Guns, Germs and Steel*, chap. 9.

62 Mazzorin and Taglizcozzo, "Morphological and Osteological Changes," in Crockford, *Dogs Through Time*, 150. The scholars concluded that "it is possible to say that a notable dimensional variety, from medium-large to small, has been present since the Neolithic and became greater in the Bronze Age. However, large dogs are present only since the Iron Age, when there seems to be an increase in the average dimensions. An even greater dimensional variability occurs in the late Roman period, when very small dogs also appear."

63 Manaserian and Antonian, "Dogs of Armenia," in Crockford, *Dogs Through Time*, 230.

64 Lupo and Janetski, "Evidence of the Domesticated Dogs," 207.

65 Azua, "Prehispanic Dog Types," in Crockford, *Dogs Through Time*, 203.

66 Azua, "Prehispanic Dog Types," in Crockford, *Dogs Through Time*, 193–94. The author of the study on Mexican dogs points out, however, that research on this is still unfolding: since "dogs were the most important animal species in Middle American civilizations, there are many studies mentioning dog remains in archaeological excavations, although as a rule few published papers go beyond the statement 'in such a place dog bones were found,' and even fewer still deal with reconstruction of organisms and identification of dog types found in archaeological sites."

67 See Diamond, *Guns, Germs, and Steel*, 159. Also see Clutton-Brock, *Natural History*: "The early stages of domestication of any species of mammal are almost always accompanied by a reduction in size of the body. This is so generally true that it is used as the main criterion to distinguish the skeletal remains of domestic from wild animals when these are retrieved by archaeological excavation of early prehistoric sites" (33–34).

68 Gray wolves range in weight from 50 to 175 pounds, with the top weight being the largest on record. The largest dog ever recorded, an English mastiff named Zorba, weighed over 340 pounds. This statistic is cited in a number of sources (including the *Guinness Book of World Records*), but can also be found in several studies of mastiffs including Klose, *English Mastiffs*. Other domesticated animals are eventually also selectively bred for increase in size—such as horses—but in their initial stages of domestication, mammals decrease in body size before humans become more complex in the selective breeding process.

69 Thurston, *Lost History*, 5–6.

70 Serpell, "From Paragon to Pariah," 250–51, mentioned breastfeeding of puppies in several different cultural settings, including among indigenous Polynesians. Gray and Young do document four specific and observed examples in "Human-Pet Dynamics," 23 (Table 3).

71 Clutton-Brock, *Natural History*, 49.

Chapter 2

1   Originally found on Great Pyrente websites. Posted on Facebook on February 18, 2013—listed as author unknown; also found on a variety of memorial pet urns and on headstones at pet cemeteries. See http://www.familypeturnsandcaskets.com/pet_poems.htm (accessed May 1, 2013).

2   A quick Google search for "news for dog memorials" yielded over 187,000,000 hits on May 4, 2013 (and similarly large numbers of hits each time I have randomly conducted this search).

3   This is the wording on one of the headstones at the pet cemetery in Hyde Park, London.

4   See Morley, *Death and the Victorians*, 211; and Howell, "Place for the Animal Dead," entire article.

5   For additional interesting discussions of death and cemeteries in Victorian England, see Hotz, *Literary Remains*, 9, 17, 76; Johnson, "Modern Cemetery"; and Strange, " 'Tho' Lost to Sight.' "

6   Howell, "Place for the Animal Dead," 9–10; londoninsight.wordpress.com.

7   There were even some people during the Victorian period who preferred the company of their dogs over those of humans in any potential afterlife. As one British attorney clearly stated when discussing his deceased retriever, "Upon the whole, I think that he was a much more exemplary character than many men and women whom I have known, and I should be very happy to meet him again in some other sphere. I would rather hunt with him on a planetoid, or a ring of Saturn, than spend my time in a narrow heaven which some zealots would arrogate to themselves and their small sect, if they could." Quoted in Howell, "Place for the Animal Dead," 13.

8   I have personally visited this cemetery. To see more images, including Rin Tin Tin's headstone, go to http://ireport.cnn.com/docs/DOC-292504 (accessed December 14, 2012).

9   To see this short film by Barbara Gordon go to http://www.youtube.com/watch?v=xU89JcJjQ4Y (accessed November 12, 2012).

10 www.petcem.com/history (accessed August 4, 2012).

11 Murphy and Haigh, *Gold Rush Dogs*, 70.

12 For more on the phenomenon of "sanitizing death," see Foucault, *Security, Territory, Population*.

13 J. D. Hill poses this question as an opening to his important essay that examines special animal deposits from Iron Age England ("Identification of Ritual Deposits," 17).

14 Davis and Valla, "Evidence for Domestication," 608–10.

15 Crockford, "Commentary on Dog Evolution," in Crockford, *Dogs Through Time*, 302. Susan Crockford, a cutting edge zooarchaeologist, makes this suggestion based on the Mallaha finding: "One of the earliest dog remains recovered is that of a young animal buried with a human female c. 12,000 years ago in Israel (Davis & Valla, 1978).

Thus, the practice of including dogs with human burials existed very early in the relationship between dogs and humans, a phenomenon that suggests an early 'role' of dogs may have been sacred or ritual rather than functional in nature. Deliberate burial of dogs on their own is also an old and geographically widespread phenomenon that transcended cultural boundaries and may be yet another manifestation of this early sacred role. Could an initial sacred role for dogs have been a natural human response to protodomestication occurring so rapidly . . . that people in all cultures were simply awed by the sudden transformation of wolves into dogs."

16 See the information in chap. 1 in this book, "Strangers No More."

17 It is important to keep in mind that zooarchaeologists make new discoveries about animals regularly, almost to the point of being overwhelmed. As they literally dig back into the evidence, some of the gaps will, in all likelihood, be filled.

18 See Graslund, "Dogs in Graves," for information on early burials in Sweden and Norway.

19 Reisner, "Dog Which Was Honored," 97.

20 While the body of the dog himself was never found, the inscription provides ample evidence of a burial according to Reisner.

21 Jackson, "Modern Cemetery," 60.

22 Cunliffe and Poole, *Danebury*, 77.

23 Hilts, "Iron Age Olives," 1.

24 K. Smith, "Guides, Guards and Gifts," 3.

25 The most accurate count I can find is 1,200 dogs discovered at Ashkelon. See Halpern, "Canine Conundrum."

26 See Wapnish and Hesse, "Pampered Pooches," 544.

27 For more about Lawrence Stager's interpretation of the Ashkelon site, see Betlyon, "People Transformed," 14. More information on Gula-Ninisina is provided in chap. 3 of this book, "Healing and Saving."

28 See Wapnish and Hesse, "Pampered Pooches" for more information on burials throughout the ancient Middle East during the same general time frame.

29 There are various descriptions of the breed for Peritas, though most likely he would have been a form of mastiff or greyhound. The city where he was buried, if indeed Plutarch's *Life of Alexander* is somewhat accurate, would likely have been in India. "It is said, too, that when he lost a dog also, named Peritas, which had been reared by him and was loved by him, he founded a city and gave it the dog's name" (Plutarch, *Life of Alexander*, 61.3, 210).

30 See Chenal-Velarde, "Food, Rituals?"

31 For a photograph of a dog's grave, see http://www.agathe.gr/id/agora/image/2004.01.2586.

32 This inscription is quoted in a variety of places, though it is difficult to trace it down to an authoritative source. The closest I can find is Mackail, *Select Epigrams*, bk. I, chap. iii, pt. vi. But it is also quoted widely

on the Internet. See, e.g., http://ancienthistory.about.com/od/anthology/ss/GreekAnthIIIf_4.htm.

33 The idea of a dog and a master (human) is one that is increasingly questioned, but probably appropriate for this context.

34 See MacKinnon and Belanger, "In Sickness and in Health."

35 Graslund, "Dogs in Graves," 168.

36 Shigehara and Hondo, "Ancient Remains of Jomon Dogs," in Crockford, *Dogs Through Time*, 62.

37 There are likely seven dogs indigenous to Japan: the shiba, akita, Hokkaido, Kishu, kai, shikoku, and Tosa.

38 See Crockford, *Practical Guide*, and Crockford, "Native Dog Types."

39 Warren, "Palaeopathology of Archaic Period Dogs," 101.

40 Barsh, Jones, and Suttles, "History, Ethnography, and Archaeology," 1. According to both oral traditions and recent archaeological discoveries, for generations the Coast Salish bred a special dog whose coat was shaved and used to weave blankets (similar to practices with sheep in many parts of the world). Some of the samples tested to confirm this connection were actually gathered by Lewis and Clark (see *Science Daily*, "Scientists Unlock the Mystery Surrounding a Tale of Shaggy Dogs," November 27, 2011). I was able to view some of these blankets at the Smithsonian's Natural History Museum.

41 Atwood, "Peru's Mummy Dogs."

42 White, *Myths of the Dog-Man*, 15.

43 As David White puts it so fittingly, "In a great number of cultures, then, the pastoral and protective role of the dog is extended beyond the world of the living into the world of the dead. Symbolically, the dog is the animal pivot of the human universe, lurking at the threshold" (*Myths of the Dog-Man*, 14–15).

44 Olsen, "Secular and Sacred Roles," in Crockford, *Dogs Through Time*, 77.

45 Olsen, "Secular and Sacred Roles," in Crockford, *Dogs Through Time*, 71.

46 Shushan, "Afterlife Conceptions," 202.

47 Kryukova, "Death as Defilement in Zoroastrianism," 80.

48 Kryukova, "Death as Defilement in Zoroastrianism," 81.

49 Day, "Dog Burials," 88.

50 See Wegner, "Beneath the Mountain-of-Anubis."

51 Nicholson, "Saqqara Dog Catacombs," 34. These catacombs were first discovered in the late nineteenth century, but they were never fully excavated. Paul Nicholson, leading a team from the University of Cardiff, has just started working on this amazing discovery again.

52 See http://www.livescience.com/13473-mummified-puppies-egyptian-dog-catacombs.html (accessed February 15, 2012). I have continued to follow carefully this news since the scale of this dig seems almost impossible. But, as of this date, the numbers being reported by the researchers are still 8 million.

53 See the fifth-century Greek epic by Nonnus, *Dionysiaca*, bk. 3, line 61; see also http://www.theoi.com/Cult/HekateCult.html: "the revelling pipes rang out a tune in honour of Hecate, divine friend of dogs."

54 Lycophron, *Alexandra*, from v. 74 (Lycophron was a Greek poet of the 3rd century BCE): "Zerynthos [on the island of Samothrake], cave of the goddess to whom dogs are slain [Hekate]."

55 Green, *Animals in Celtic Life and Myth*, 112.

56 White, *Myths of the Dog-Man*, 14.

57 It is depicted in the painting "Attachment" by Sir Edwin Landseer (widely recognized as the most prominent dog painter in 19th-century Britain). Landseer is also the artist who painted "The Old Shepherd's Chief Mourner."

58 The story of Gough's dog played well in the Romantic period. Some newspaper reports suggested that the little dog had taken to eating the remains of her owner, but other reports denied this and attributed the body's decay to ravens. Regardless, it is the sentiment of the dog as faithful companion even after death that comes through quite clearly in the artistic representations of this event. See also *The Guardian*, Friday, March 14, 2003, http://www.guardian.co.uk/artanddesign/2003/mar/15/art.artsfeatures (accessed April 14, 2013).

59 Wordsworth, *Complete Poetical Works*, 385. The quotation is just the last stanza of the poem, which can be found in its entirety in most of the major collections of Wordsworth's works.

60 This story was retold in an Americanized version in the movie *Hachi: A Dog's Tale* (Sony 2009).

61 See Turner, *Hachiko Waits*.

62 In the contemporary electronic world, pet memorials are often associated with the "Rainbow Bridge"—a poem that is shared by dog lovers on the Internet all over the world. Usually marked as "author unknown," the poem might have first been published in the 1994 book *Legend of the Rainbow Bridge* by William Britton.

63 Ambros, *Bones of Contention*, chap. 4, "Necrogeography."

64 Ambros, *Bones of Contention*, 4–5.

65 Ambros, *Bones of Contention*, 192.

66 See Morris, "Managing Pet Owners' Guilt." There are also numerous websites and blogs that try to provide an outlet for owners after they choose to euthanize a pet.

67 See http://www.hbo.com/documentaries/one-nation-under-dog-stories -of-fear-loss-and-betrayal/index.html (accessed November 8, 2012).

68 See HBO website. http://www.hbo.com/documentaries/one-nation -under-dog-stories-of-fear-loss-and-betrayal/index.html.

69 Brandes, "Meaning," 101.

Chapter 3

1 Jennings, *What a Difference a Dog Makes*, 2.

2   See dogsdetectcancer.org for more information.

3   McCulloch et al., "Diagnostic Accuracy," 30.

4   This research is documented in too many places to cite. For ease, see Tyson, "Dogs' Dazzling Sense."

5   Tyson, "Dogs' Dazzling Sense."

6   While writing this chapter, I'm fostering a mom and her puppies. It is urgent to keep them from getting an upper-respiratory infection that clogs their noses in the first couple of weeks because then they are unable to eat and will very likely starve to death without significant assistance.

7   This is true of cats as well; likely even other companion animals, as tests are showing.

8   From the thirteenth-century *Aberdeen Bestiary*, Text f19v. The entire text can be found online at http://www.abdn.ac.uk/bestiary/translat/19v .hti. A similar saying is found in French, *Langue de chien, langue de médecin* ("A dog's tongue is a doctor's tongue").

9   There are many interpretations of this passage, including one that equates the compassion of the dogs with the compassion of Gentiles over against the cruelty of the rich man.

10 Gula was also known as Ninisina or "Lady of Isin" or as Ninkarrak. Sumerian is the language category, and Babylon is the name of the ancient nation-state, located in present-day Iraq.

11 For examples of these images go to the "Ancient Mesopotamian Gods and Goddesses" project at the University of Pennsylvania: http://oracc .museum.upenn.edu/amgg/listofdeities/gulaninkarrak/ (accessed February 9, 2013).

12 Halpern, "Canine Conundrum," 135. He also notes that her name at Lagash in Iraq—Bawa/Baba—might be onomatopoeic for a dog's bark.

13 Isin was located approximately 200 kilometers south-southeast of Baghdad (Ornan, "Goddess Gula," 13).

14 See Ornan, "Goddess Gula," 14.

15 These images are often on stamp or cylinder seals used to make impressions in clay (which was the medium for writing in the cuneiform script before papyrus and leather were used).

16 Halpern, "Canine Conundrum," 134. Some of the text cited is damaged, but scholars have reconstructed it in the form quoted here.

17 Black and Green, *Gods, Demons and Symbols*, 70.

18 See Yuhong, "Rabies and Rabid Dogs," for information about rabies in Sumerian literature.

19 Collins, "Puppy in Hittite Ritual," 214.

20 See Hart and Powell, "Antibacterial Properties of Saliva."

21 Manaserian and Antonian, "Dogs of Armenia," in Crockford, *Dogs Through Time*, 230.

22 Oaths taken by physicians and signs for many medical items and places still carry a symbol of Asklepios.

23 Legends vary throughout the Hellenistic world regarding the nativity

and childhood stories of Asklepios. In the area around Epidauros, dogs are sacred and more frequently included in these legends.

24 A. Walton, *Cult of Asklepios*, 65–66.

25 Strelan, *Paul, Artemis*, 149.

26 Quoted in Strelan, *Paul, Artemis*, 150.

27 Aelian, *On the Characteristics of Animals*, 7.13 (Greek natural history, 2nd–3rd century CE).

28 See chap. 2 in this book, "Journey to the Afterlife."

29 See Halpern, "Canine Conundrum," and Stager, "Why Were Hundreds of Dogs Buried at Ashkelon?." It is quite conceivable that this connection exists since the cult of Asklepios was achieving prominence for the first time in the fifth century BCE as well. So a Greek cultural translation between ancient Babylonian (and Neo-Babylonian) sources to the Phoenician-influenced world of Ashkelon is quite probable.

30 For more information see chap. 2 in this book, "Journey to the Afterlife."

31 MacKinnon and Belanger, "In Sickness and in Health," 43.

32 Green, *Symbol and Image*, 28–29.

33 See Jenkins, "Role of the Dog."

34 Green, *Symbol and Image*, 200–201.

35 I have interviewed people in the area around Guignefort's tomb, including the current president of the Saint Guignefort Society, Jean-Louis Maret. See http://www.association-saint-guignefort.fr/ for more information. It is also interesting to note that this same basic story line of a dog saving a child and then being unjustly killed is found in a legend in India, which is translated into Arabic.

36 Roch's story can be found in a number of places, including McBrien, *Lives of the Saints*, 333–34; Cross, *Oxford Dictionary of the Christian Church*, 1192; Koenig-Briker, *365 Saints*, 229; Catholic Online's directory of saints, http://www.catholic.org/saints/saint.php?saint_id=156; and in most guides to Catholic saints.

37 It is likely that this round of the plague led to the end of Venice's centrality to commercial life in the Mediterranean.

38 "A Helping Hound" is the title of a small article in the journal *Mental Health Practice*.

39 This is an old saying, author unknown.

40 The city of London eventually beat out Austin, Texas, for this *Guinness Book of World Records* designation.

41 Friedmann et al., "Animal Companions."

42 Neal, "Trained Dogs," 65.

43 A few of the more prominent studies are Hall and Malpus, "Pets as Therapy"; Friedmann et al., "Animal Companions"; Allen, Blascovich, and Mendes, "Cardiovascular Reactivity"; Bauman et al., "Epidemiology of Dog Walking."

44 See Montague, "Continuing Care."

45 For more information, see Alzheimer's Scotland and Dogs for the Disabled.

46 This organization was formerly called the Delta Society. See http://www.petpartners.org/.

47 Kwong and Bartholomew, "Not Just a Dog," 434.

48 See the Centers for Disease Control report, http://www.cdc.gov/ncbddd/autism/data.html (accessed March 1, 2013).

49 Smyth and Slevin, "Experiences of Family Life."

50 See http://www.puppiesbehindbars.com/home.

51 Kwong and Bartholomew, "Not Just a Dog," 421.

52 See the *Huffington Post*, "Newtown Therapy Dogs Headed to Boston to Provide Comfort in Wake of Boston Marathon Attack," April 16, 2013. http://www.huffingtonpost.com/2013/04/16/newtown-dogs-boston_n_3093840.html (accessed April 22, 2013).

53 See the Search Dog Foundation's website, http://www.searchdogfoundation.org/.

54 See the story online at Environmental Graffiti, http://www.environmentalgraffiti.com/animals/news-four-legged-hereos-911ground-zero?image=23.

55 See Bauer, *Dog Heroes of September 11*, for a series of stories about 9/11 rescue and therapy dogs. There were some controversies about the September 11 dogs, including whether they should have been sent into such a dangerous site. Some of the dogs suffered the same types of negative health effects experienced by the first responders after the World Trade Center towers fell (220).

Chapter 4

1 Petraeus made this remark while commander of U.S. forces in Afghanistan. See Forer, "Osama Bin Laden Raid."

2 "Military war dog" is the official name of trained combat dogs by the U.S. military. Current news about the dogs can be found in a variety of places, including http://www.uswardogs.org/.

3 The entire idea of other humans as targets, and executing missions in this manner, is difficult and problematic; it is one of the many issues that make this particular relationship with dogs controversial.

4 A number of books have been written in the last decade about military war dogs in the United States, so this broad history is covered fairly well. For more information, see Goodavage, *Soldier Dogs*; Lemish, *War Dogs*; Rogak, *Dogs of War*; Dowling, *Sergeant Rex*.

5 A documentary was released on Animal Planet in February 2013 titled *Glory Hounds*. This quotation is from that documentary. See http://www.channelguidemagblog.com/index.php/2013/02/21/animal-planet-glory-hounds-military-dogs/.

6 See Lobell and Powell, "Dogs of Roman Britain," 31.

7 This is approximately the same time period when dogs associated with the goddess Gula emerged in the same part of the world.

8 At this point in Mesopotamia the equids were likely ass/onager hybrids, not an animal that is exactly like a modern-day horse. See Clutton-Brock, *Natural History*, chap. 10.

9 Tsouparopoulou, "'K-9 Corps' of the Third Dynasty," 10.

10 Tutankhamun's "Painted Box," noted by the archaeologists who first discovered the Pharoah's tomb in the 1920s as one of the most magnificent pieces of art recovered, is currently housed at the Cairo Museum. See http://www.nilemuse.com/muse/TutBoxF.html for images.

11 See Polyaenus, *Stratagems of War*, bk. 7, chap. 9; also quoted in Forster, "Dogs in Ancient Warfare."

12 Forster, "Dogs in Ancient Warfare," 115.

13 It is important to note here that various Greek-culture groups were at war with each other and using dogs against each other. There were various rising and falling Mediterranean and western Asian powers during this ancient period. The Peloponnesian War is just one example of this infighting. See Forster, "Dogs in Ancient Warfare."

14 Aelian, *Various Histories* 14.46. Available online at http://penelope.uchicago.edu/aelian/varhist14.html.

15 This type of dog likely came from the Molossis people who lived in the mountains of northwestern Greece and southern Albania. Other dog breeds that have some genetic connection to Molossians are the St. Bernard, Great Pyrenees, Newfoundland, and Bernese Mountain dog.

16 From the Augustan poet Grattius, *Cynegetica*; quoted on the University of Chicago *Encyclopedia Romana* website, http://penelope.uchicago.edu/~grout/encyclopaedia_romana/miscellanea/canes/canes.html. See also Hull, *Hounds and Hunting*.

17 See Karunanithy, "War Dogs," 19. See also Saint Patrick's *Confession*, chap. 19.

18 For a series of interesting accounts of Civil War dogs, see Zucchero, *Loyal Hearts*.

19 See Lanting, "Dogs in the Civil War."

20 This story is recounted in multiple places. Images of the monument and accounts of Sallie's bravery can be found online at www.fallendogs.com, www.nycivilwar.us/sallie.html, and numerous other sites.

21 Stubby, or at least his taxidermic stuffed version, is on display at the Smithsonian's National Museum of American History. He had been held in storage at the museum for years before being refurbished and placed on display again. I was able to visit the display and see Stubby, and I encourage readers to do the same. More information on him and images of the display can be found on the Smithsonian's website, http://amhistory.si.edu/militaryhistory/collection/object.asp?ID=15&back=1 (accessed March 12, 2013).

22 See Downey, *Dogs for Defense*, for a complete history.

23 See Ewers, "Dogs of War," 12. This is part of the official communication about Caesar's actions: "Caesar (a German shepherd) was the only means of communication between M Company and Second Battalion CP, carrying messages, overlays, and captured Jap papers. On [the second day], M Co's telephone lines were cut and Caesar was again the only means of communication. Caesar was wounded on the morning of D plus 2 and had to be carried back to the Regimental CP on a stretcher, but he had already established himself as a hero." See Kelly, "Government Asked for Pets."

24 There are interesting accounts of dogs overturning their sleds and stubbornly returning to base during training runs because the human handler was not experienced and mistreated them. See Fischer, "Training Sled Dogs," 17.

25 Fischer, "Training Sled Dogs," 18.

26 Fischer, "Training Sled Dogs," 19.

27 See Ruark, "Have the War Dogs." The reference to a dog biting a general is about "Chips," who "stormed a pillbox, helped to capture four Nazis . . . and then bit General Eisenhower," briefly recorded in Ruark's article.

28 See "Always Faithful," a short video documentary of the installation of the memorial. There is another feature-length documentary by the same name that focuses on dogs and their handlers in the wars in Iraq and Afghanistan. See https://www.facebook.com/alwaysfaithfulmovie for information on that documentary.

29 Quoted in the *Daily Mail*: http://www.dailymail.co.uk/news/article -1302677/Judy-dogged-PoW-defied-Japanese.html.

30 There are a number of reports that provide a detailed account of the life of this amazing dog, including Varley, *Judy Story*; Long, *Animal Heroes*; and the *Daily Mail* account just cited.

31 There is a large Vietnam Dog Handler Association that is still active and has over 2,000 members. See http://vdha.us/ for the most recent information.

32 Lemish, *War Dogs*, xi.

33 See Ruark, "Have the War Dogs," 93.

34 See Dao, "After Duty."

35 http://www.lifewithdogs.tv/2012/04/british-government-euthanizes -800-war-dogs/.

36 See Douglass, *Narrative*, 85.

37 See Douglass, "Farewell to the British People," 1.

38 See Lapham, "Baumer Phase Dog Burial"; and Werner, "Dog Tails."

39 It is worth noting that the Fuegian dog, now extinct, has a particularly interesting and complicated lineage. As Clutton-Brock explains, the "phonetic characters of the genus fall between those of the species of *canis* and the true foxes . . . *Vulpes*" ("Man-Made Dogs," 1340–42). They are in something of an intermediate state. With this in mind, the Fuegian dog is sometimes compared to the Australian dingo. Eventually,

according to Clutton-Brock, indigenous South Americans preferred the more highly socialized European dog, but this does not negate the aboriginal Fuegian dog as an interesting domesticated hybrid-type canine.

40 See Schwartz, *History of Dogs,* chap. 1; Allison et al., "Pre-Columbian Dog"; and Allen, *Dogs of the American Aborigines,* 493–94.

41 See Allen, *Dogs of the American Aborigines.* There is a different chapter on each specific dog type in this book.

42 Las Casas, *Devastation of the Indies,* 127.

43 These wars cannot be severed from the history of slavery in the U.S. and the Caribbean, or from the genocide that resulted from the centuries-long practice of importing slaves from West Africa.

44 Native American inhabitants of areas throughout the United States continue to fight for their land into the twenty-first century.

45 J. Campbell, "Seminoles," 267.

46 See J. Campbell, "Seminoles," for an interesting historical analysis.

47 Digital file available from the Library of Congress, cph 3b36096: http://hdl.loc.gov/loc.pnp/cph.3b36096.

48 See King, "Letter from Birmingham Jail," 186.

49 See Skabelund, *Empire of Dogs,* for a fascinating study of this entire process.

50 See Sims, "*Dog Map of the World.*"

51 This theory is still contested. Some attribute the megafauna extinctions to climate change alone, others to human (and possibly human-dog) hunting in these newly human-inhabited areas. The extinctions might also have been caused by a combination of both factors. See Fiedel, "Man's Best Friend," for an interesting theory about the megafauna extinctions in North America after humans first arrived in the Americas with dogs.

52 See Diamond, *Guns, Germs and Steel,* 42–46. Others suggest that dog-human hunting teams were just one factor among many, a kind of perfect storm. See Wroe et al., "Megafaunal Extinction."

53 The date of 10,000 years before the present is controversial because that could suggest that this is the oldest evidence for dogs in North America. See Torben et al., "Dogs, Humans," 1082.

54 This removal was carried out by the National Park Service and the U.S. Navy. In addition to disturbing other species' breeding grounds, dogs also brought canine diseases that affected the native foxes on the islands. See Torben et al., "Dogs, Humans."

55 When I visited the Galapagos Islands for research, I was immediately struck to see dogs who obviously were not intended for that climate. A Siberian husky greeted me around one corner and an American Eskimo around another.

56 Barnett, "Eradication and Control," 359.

57 There is likely an even more dramatic impact on native wildlife by cats who also accompanied humans to the Galapagos.

58 Versions of this same interpretation can be found in Exodus Rabbah and Rashi. I am particularly grateful to Ken Stone ("Dogs of Exodus") and Aaron Gross ("Question of the Creature") for their work on Levinas in this area.

59 Levinas, "Name of a Dog," 153.

Chapter 5

1 Shelley, *Frankenstein*, 187.

2 I designate them "at risk" here because of the combination of being "pit bulls" and having a disability.

3 For more information, go to http://www.petpartners.org/.

4 See https://www.facebook.com/stevie.wonder.dog for more information. Stevie has also been featured by the Stubby Dog Project, http://stubbydog.org/2012/03/stevie-the-wonder-dog/, and I'm Not A Monster, http://imnotamonster.org/work/stevie-salt-lake-city-ut/ (all websites accessed January 12, 2013).

5 See http://www.npr.org/blogs/thisisnpr/2013/02/20/172414910/top-dog-takes-national-pet-radio-contest.

6 See Banerjee, "Home Is Where Mamma Is," 5. Other interesting interpretations that shed light on thinking about the dog-human relationship are: Gilbert and Gubar, "Horror's Twin"; J. Smith, "'Cooped Up'"; Mellor, *Mary Shelley*.

7 Sutter and Ostrander, "Dog Star Rising." This fact is pointed out in a variety of sources and is a central point in the argument regarding the human-dog connection.

8 For a wonderful overview of this process in terms of human evolution, see Diamond, *Guns, Germs and Steel*, chap. 1.

9 See J. K. Walton, "Mad Dogs," 219. Also see Kete, *Best in the Boudoir*, 64–66. Kete provides a history of the first naturalists in England and France using specific "varieties" for dogs. The first record is in 1788 when Georges-Louis Leclerc de Buffon suggested fourteen "varieties of dogs" (64). His classification was followed by a series of other systems. While these late eighteenth-century lists are the precursors to the kennel clubs of the nineteenth century, as early as the sixteenth century some classifications had taken place. For example, Johannes Caius listed seventeen varieties of dogs from the Tudor period in British history—"Terrar, Harier, Bloudhound, Gasehunde, Grehound, leuiner, Tumber, Stealer, Setter, Water Spaniel or Fynder, Land Spaniel, Spaniel-gentle or Comforter, Shepherd's Dog, Mastive or Bande-Dog, Wappe, Turnspit, Dancer" (*Of English Dogs*, 13).

10 Ritvo, *Animal Estate*, does a wonderful job describing, in detail, this entire evolution of the idea of dog breeding and fancying; see chap. 2. See also J. K. Walton, "Mad Dogs," 219.

11 See the pamphlet by Plumb for more information on this overall phenomenon, particularly p. 10.

12 Various histories report this as the first dog show, including the official website of the Kennel Club of the U.K.: http://www.thekennelclub.org .uk/kchistory (accessed January 22, 2013).

13 Ritvo, *Animal Estate*, 98.

14 Leroy and Baumung, "Mating Practices," 66. The authors are quoting a study by Cathryn Mellersh, "Give a Dog a Genome," published in 2008 in *Veterinary Journal* (London).

15 Various studies have shown this, but for a recent claim, see the National Institutes of Health Study, "Variants in Three Genes Account for Most Dog Coat Differences," August 27, 2009. http://www.nih.gov/news/ health/aug2009/nhgri-27.htm (accessed January 13, 2013).

16 Giant George, a seven-foot long, 252-pound Great Dane, is the longest dog currently living. For more information on George, see Nasser, *Giant George.*

17 Jeremy Shearman and Alan Wilton describe the genetic intrigue of dogs in their "Origins of the Domestic Dog," 1–7.

18 See Sutter and Ostrander, "Dog Star Rising."

19 The term "lethal white" has been appropriated for use in dog circles, though it actually refers to a condition in horses that frequently results in the death of the foal within a few days.

20 This term and the genetics associated with it apply to any dogs who come with merle coloring—Great Danes, dachshunds, Catahoula leopard dogs, collies, Border collies, and shelties.

21 For more information, go to the Australian Shepherd Health and Genetics Institute, http://www.ashgi.org/articles/color_troub_merle. htm (accessed January 20, 2013).

22 See Denizet-Lewis, "Can the Bulldog Be Saved?" where James Serpell makes this claim.

23 For more information, see both the American Society for the Prevention of Cruelty to Animals (ASPCA) and the Humane Society of the United States (HSUS).

24 See the Humane Society of the United States, *An Advocate's Guide*, 1.

25 See http://www.govtrack.us/congress/bills/113/hr847#overview.

26 See Ritvo, *Animal Estate*, 107–13, for an account of both the demise and the reestablishment of the bulldog in Great Britain during the nineteenth century.

27 Shelley, *Frankenstein*, 93.

28 The American pit bull terrier (APBT) is recognized by the United Kennel Club (http://www.ukcdogs.com/Web.nsf/Breeds/AmericanPitBull Terrier12012012; accessed August 13, 2013), but not the American Kennel Club. Regardless, when a dog is, sometimes randomly, labeled a "pit bull," she or he could be from a wide range of dog breed mixes.

29 There are several websites that have a "can you spot the pit bull" test: http://nationalcanineresearchcouncil.com/uploaded_files/tinymce/ Pit%20Bull%20ID%20Poster.pdf (accessed August 12, 2013); http:// www.understand-a-bull.com/Findthebull/findpitbull_v3.html (accessed

August 12, 2013); http://heathercherry.blogspot.com/2009/06/can-you
-spot-pit-bull.html (accessed August 12, 2013).

30 See D. M. Campbell, "Pit Bull Bans," for more information on the current state of BSL.

31 See   http://www.examiner.com/article/pit-bulls-and-euthanasia-rates;
also Twining, Arluke, and Patronek, "Managing the Stigma."

32 The CDC website provides helpful information. See http://www.cdc
.gov/HomeandRecreationalSafety/Dog-Bites/index.html

33 National Canine Research Council, "The Problems with Dog Bite Studies," 1.

34 For more information on dog-bite studies, see the National Canine
Research Council's website, http://www.nationalcanineresearchcouncil
.com/dogbites/whatisadogbite/ (accessed August 12, 2013).

35 The pit bull is the only dog breed/type to appear on the cover of *Life*
three times.

36 When the Bulldog Club was formed in Britain in 1874, in an attempt
to keep the breed from going extinct, its own pamphlet described the
dog as "much maligned and . . . very little understood" (Ritvo, *Animal
Estate*, 111).

37 For an account of the aftermath of the rescue of these dogs, see Gorant,
Lost Dogs.

38 More information about this disease can be found on the University
of Pennsylvania's website: http://cal.vet.upenn.edu/projects/dxendopar/
parasitepages/protozoa/babesiagibs.html (accessed August 13, 2013).

39 See information on this at the Best Friends Animal Sanctuary site: http://
bfla.bestfriends.org/10/post/2012/07/michael-vicks-dog-adoption-app
.html. Michael Vick has also just published a book telling his story from
a different perspective, *Finally Free: An Autobiography*.

40 See Twining, Arluke, and Patronek, "Managing the Stigma" for a careful analysis of breed stigma.

Chapter 6

1 Christine, on her Great Pyrenees dog (Facebook, July 2012). Tillie was
a lovely Great Pyrenees who lived for a brief, but meaningful, time with
Christine and her family.

2 This is the newspaper for Austin, Texas—the state capital.

3 *Austin American-Statesman*, "Welcome to Dogtown."

4 Books such as Katz, *New Work of Dogs*; and Homans, *What's a Dog
For?* explore this assumption and, to a certain extent, make this claim
as well.

5 See Katz, *New Work of Dogs*; Homans, *What's a Dog For?*

6 *Rig Veda*, 44.

7 http://dog-church.com/about/ (accessed April 25, 2013; no longer
available).

8 See Croland, "Dogs Go to Church."

9   See Hobgood-Oster, *The Friends We Keep*, 182–93; and idem, *Holy Dogs and Asses*, chap. 6, for a more complete history of the blessings of animals in Christianity.

10 Stephen Webb, a theologian who has written extensively on human-animal relationships, including his book *On God and Dogs*, finds this interpretation of dogs as religious subjects, and humans as religiously connected with dogs in very specific ways, less than completely convincing. In his fascinating theological piece, he suggests that humans are to dogs as God is to humans. Humans are totally in control of dogs, and they are beholden to humans. This lack of any agency on the part of dogs is, in my estimation, a misunderstanding of their role in human history and places too much emphasis on human dominion.

11 See Oppenheimer, "Churches Take Steps."

12 The name of the organization is connected to St. Martin de Porres, a Peruvian saint who established a dog and cat sanctuary in Lima in the seventeenth century.

13 While this is incorrect grammatically, it is a bumper sticker/window magnet commonly seen on the cars of people who participate in dog rescue efforts.

14 Poem by the author. This poem was written and submitted to a competition for funding for a not-for-profit dog rescue group in 2012.

15 To be fully forthcoming, the author admits that her license plate is DOG RSQ.

16 The debate about dogs as property, or as more or other than property, continues in the legal system. Their status varies wildly. In some states and nations they are beings who have emotional value, in other states/nations they are property with a mere dollar value.

17 See Descartes, *Philosophical Essays*. While Descartes' opinion on animals is reflected in many places in these letters, two specific pieces are in his "Letter to the Marquis of Newcastle: About Animals" (275–77) and "Letter to More, 5 February 1649" (292–96).

18 See http://www.humanesociety.org/issues/pet_overpopulation/ for statistics. Most statistics include both dogs and cats, so it is difficult to get accurate figures. For percentage of euthanized animals, see http://www.statisticbrain.com/animal-shelter-statistics/.

19 There are numerous accounts of animal rescue in the aftermath of Katrina, so I will not recount the entire story here. For more information, see the film *Dark Water Rising*; Meadows, *Hurricane Katrina Animal Rescue*; Best Friends, *Not Left Behind*; Scott, *Pawprints of Katrina*.

20 This fact is made apparent in the current debates about the legal status of pets—are they property or do they hold emotional value, at the very least? The Texas Supreme Court, e.g., ruled in April 2013 that dogs are merely property. See http://www.examiner.com/article/texas-supreme-court-ruling-treats-dogs-as-property.

21 See Anderman's *New York Times* article, "Full Circle," for a report on Emmylou Harris' animal rescue efforts.

22 See Jamison, Wenk, and Parker's essay, "Every Sparrow That Falls," for an analysis of the ways that animal rights activism functions as a religion for some people.

23 The definitions of religion vary widely. For a solid and widely accepted functional definition, see Geertz's seminal essay, "Religion as a Cultural System."

24 See Harbolt, *Bridging the Bond.*

25 Interviews conducted by the author during 2012 with rescuers throughout the United States.

26 Roth, *Man Who Talks to Dogs*, xviii.

27 The category of "pet" is one that is contested by advocates of many "pets" (dogs, cats, horses, ferrets, etc.) for a variety of complicated reasons—it implies property and ownership, frivolity, oppressive power structure issues, and more.

Bibliography

Aberdeen Bestiary. Aberdeen University Library MS 24. http://www
.abdn.ac.uk/bestiary/intro.hti.

Aelian. *Claudius Aelianus: His Various History*, book 14. Translated
by Thomas Stanley, 1665. http://penelope.uchicago.edu/aelian/
varhist14.html.

———. *On the Characteristics of Animals*. Translated by A. Schol-
field. Cambridge: Cambridge University Press, 1959.

Allen, Glover. *Dogs of the American Aborigines*. Bulletin of the
Museum of Comparative Zoology (Cambridge, Mass: Harvard
University, 1920).

Allen, K., J. Blascovich, and W. B. Mendes. "Cardiovascular Reactivity and the Presence of Pets, Friends, and Spouses: The Truth
about Cats and Dogs." *Psychosomatic Medicine* 64 (2002):
727–39.

Allison, Marvin, Guillermo Focacci, and Calogero Santoro. "The
Pre-Columbian Dog from Arica, Chile." *American Journal of
Physical Anthropology* 59, no. 3 (1982): 299–304.

"Always Faithful." http://www.dpca.org/Legisltv/AlwaysFaithful
.htm.

Ambros, Barbara. *Bones of Contention: Animals and Religion in
Contemporary Japan*. Honolulu: University of Hawai'i Press,
2012.

———. "The Necrogeography of Pet Memorial Spaces: Pets as Lim-
inal Family Members in Contemporary Japan." *Material Religion* 6, no. 3 (2010): 304–35.

Anderman, Joan. "A Full Circle for Emmylou Harris." *New York Times*, March 22, 2013.

l'Association Saint Guignefort. *Saint Guignefort: Légende, Archéologie, Histoire*. Châtillon-sur-Chalaronne, 2005.

Atwood, Roger. "Peru's Mummy Dogs." *Archaeology Archive* 60, no. 1 (2007). http://archive.archaeology.org/0701/abstracts/peru.html (accessed April 4, 2012).

Austin American-Statesman. "Welcome to Dogtown." February 17, 2013. http://www.statesman.com/news/lifestyles/pets/welcome-to-dogtown-aka-austin-texas/nWPZb/.

Axelsson, Erik, Abhirami Ratnakumar, Maja-Louise Arendt, Khurram Maqbool, Matthew T. Webster, Michele Perloski, Olof Liberg, Jon M. Arnemo, Åke Hedhammar, and Kerstin Lindblad-Toh. "The Genomic Signature of Dog Domestication Reveals Adaptation to a Starch-Rich Diet." *Nature* online. January 23, 2013. http://www.nature.com/nature/journal/vaop/ncurrent/full/nature11837.html (accessed February 25, 2013).

Azua, Raul Valadez. "Prehispanic Dog Types in Middle America." In Crockford, *Dogs Through Time*, 193–204.

Banerjee, Suparna. "Home Is Where Mamma Is: Reframing the Science Question in *Frankenstein*." *Women's Studies: An Interdisciplinary Journal* 40, no. 1 (2010): 1–22.

Barnett, Bruce. "Eradication and Control of Feral and Free-Ranging Dogs in the Galapagos Islands." *Proceedings of the Twelfth Vertebrate Pest Conference*, 1986. http://digitalcommons.unl.edu/vpc12/8/ (accessed July 8, 2013).

Barsh, R. L., J. M. Jones, and W. Suttles. "History, Ethnography, and Archaeology of the Coast Salish Woolly-Dog." In *Dogs and People in Social, Working, Economic or Symbolic Interaction*, edited by L. M. Snyder and E. A. Moore, 1–11. Oxford: Oxbow, 2006.

Bauer, Nona Kilgore. *Dog Heroes of September 11: A Tribute to America's Search and Rescue Dogs*. Allenhurst, N.J.: Kennel Club Books, 2006.

Bauman A. E., S. J. Russell, S. E. Furber, and A. J. Dobson, "The Epidemiology of Dog Walking." *Medical Journal of Australia* 175 (2001): 632–34.

Bekoff, Marc. *The Emotional Lives of Animals*. Novato, Calif.: New World Library, 2007.

———. "PTSD in War Dogs Finally Getting the Attention It Deserves." *Psychology Today*, December 2, 2011.

Benecke, Norbert. "Studies on Early Dog Remains from Northern Europe." *Journal of Archaeological Science* 14 (1987): 31–49.

Best Friends Animal Society and Troy Snow. *Not Left Behind: Rescuing the Pets of New Orleans.* Toronto: Yorkville Press, 2006.

Betlyon, John. "A People Transformed: Palestine in the Persian Period." *Near Eastern Archaeology* 68, nos. 1–22 (2005): 4–58.

Black, Jeremy, and Anthony Green. *Gods, Demons and Symbols of Ancient Mesopotamia: An Illustrated Dictionary.* Austin: University of Texas Press, 2003.

Bower, Bruce. "World's Oldest Dog Debated." *Discovery News*, July 23, 2010.

Bowron, E. P., Carolyn Rose Rebbert, Robert Rosenblum, and William Secord. *Best in Show: The Dog in Art from the Renaissance to Today.* New Haven: Yale University Press, 2006.

Brandes, Stanley. "The Meaning of American Pet Cemetery Gravestones." *Ethnology* 48, no. 2 (2009): 99–118.

Britton, William. *The Legend of the Rainbow Bridge.* Savannah, Tenn.: Savannah Publishing, 2011.

Brodie, Sarah, and Francis Biley. "An Exploration of the Potential Benefits of Pet-Facilitated Therapy." *Journal of Clinical Nursing* 8, no. 4 (1999): 329–37.

Caius, Johannes. *Of English Dogs.* Translated by Abraham Flemming. Alton, U.K.: Beech Publishing House, 1576. Repr. Warwickshire: Vintage Dog Books, 2005. Originally in Latin.

Campbell, Dana M. "Pit Bull Bans: The State of Breed-Specific Legislation." *GPSolo* 26, no. 5 (2009): 36–41.

Campbell, John. "The Seminoles, the 'Bloodhound War,' and Abolitionism, 1796–1865." *Journal of Southern History* 72, no. 2 (2006): 259–302.

Capp, Dawn M. *American Pit Bull Terriers: Fact or Fiction. The Truth Behind One of America's Most Popular Breeds.* Irvine, Calif.: Doral Publishing, 2004.

Chenal-Velarde, Isabelle. "Food, Rituals? The Exploitation of Dogs from Eretria (Greece) during the Helladic and Hellenistic Periods." In *Dogs and People in Social, Working, Economic or Symbolic Interaction*, edited by L. M. Snyder and E. A. Moore, 24–31. Oxford: Oxbow, 2006.

Chidester, David. "Darwin's Dogs." *Soundings: An Interdisciplinary Journal* (Spring/Summer 2009): 51–79.

Clark, David. "On Being the Last Kantian in Nazi Germany: Dwelling with Animals after Levinas." *Postmodernism and the Ethical Subject* (2004): 41–74.

Clottes, Jean. "Chauvet Cave (ca. 30,000 B.C.)." In *Heilbrunn Timeline of Art History*. New York: The Metropolitan Museum of Art, 2000.

Clutton-Brock, Juliet. "Introduction." In Crockford, *Dogs Through Time*, 3–7.

———. *A Natural History of Domesticated Mammals*. Cambridge: Cambridge University Press: 1999.

———. "Origins of the Dog: Domestication and Early History." In *The Domestic Dog: Its Evolution, Behaviour and Interactions with People*, edited by James Serpell, 7–20. Cambridge: Cambridge University Press, 1995.

———. "Man-Made Dogs." *Science* 197 (1977): 1340–42.

Clutton-Brock, J., and A. C. Kitchener. "An Anomalous Wolf, *Canis Lupus Arctos*, from Ellesmere Island and the Problem of Hybridisation between Wild and Domestic Canids." In Crockford, *Dogs Through Time*, 257–69.

Cohen, Mark E. *Cultic Calendars of the Ancient Near East*. Bethesda, Md.: Capital Decisions, 1993.

Collins, Billie Jean. "The Puppy in Hittite Ritual." *Journal of Cuneiform Studies* 42, no. 2 (1990): 211–26.

Coppinger, Raymond, and Lorna Coppinger. *Dogs: A Startling New Understanding of Canine Origin, Behavior and Evolution*. New York: Scribner, 2001.

Coren, Stanley. *The Intelligence of Dogs: Canine Consciousness and Capabilities*. New York: Free Press, 1994.

———. *The Pawprints of History: Dogs and the Course of Human Events*. New York: Free Press, 2002.

Crockford, Susan. "A Commentary on Dog Evolution: Regional Variation, Breed Development and Hybridisation with Wolves." In Crockford, *Dogs Through Time*, 295–312.

———. "Dog Evolution: A Role for Thyroid Hormone Physiology in Domestication Changes." In Crockford, *Dogs Through Time*, 11–20.

———, ed. *Dogs Through Time: An Archaeological Perspective*. Oxford: Archaeopress, 2008.

———. "Native Dog Types in North America before Arrival of European Dogs." Presented at the 30th World Congress of the World Small Animal Veterinary Association, May 2005. http://www.vin.com/proceedings/Proceedings.plx?CID=WSAVA2005&PID=11071&O=Generic.

———. *A Practical Guide to In Situ Dog Remains for the Field Archaeologist*. Victoria, B.C.: Pacific Identifications, 2009.

Croland, Michael. "Dogs Go to Church." In *The Revealer: A Daily Review of Religion and Media*. May 13, 2010. http://therevealer. org/archives/4113 (accessed August 13, 2013).

Cross, F. L. *The Oxford Dictionary of the Christian Church*. Oxford: Oxford University Press, 1983.

Cunliffe, Barry, and Cynthia Poole. *Danebury: An Iron Age Hillfort in Hampshire*. Council for British Archaeology Research Report 73 (1991).

Dale-Green, Patricia. "The Healing Lick and Rabid Bite." *British Homeopathic Journal* 53, no. 1 (1964): 51–59.

Dao, James. "After Duty, Dogs Suffer Like Soldiers." *New York Times*, December 1, 2011.

Dark Water Rising. Shidog Films, 2006.

Davis, Simon, and François Valla. "Evidence for Domestication of the Dog 12,000 Years Ago in the Natufian of Israel." *Nature* 276 (1978): 608–10.

Day, Leslie Preston. "Dog Burials in the Greek World." *American Journal of Archaeology* 88, no. 1 (1984): 21–32.

Delise, Karen. *The Pit Bull Placebo: The Media, Myths and Politics of Canine Aggression*. n.p.: Anubis Publishing, 2007.

Denizet-Lewis, Benoit. "Can the Bulldog Be Saved?" *New York Times*, November 22, 2011.

Derr, Mark. *Dog's Best Friend*. Chicago: University of Chicago Press, 2004.

Descartes, René. *Philosophical Essays and Correspondence*. Edited by R. Ariew. Indianapolis: Hackett, 2000.

Diamond, Jared. *Guns, Germs and Steel*. New York: Norton, 1999.

Doniger, Wendy, ed. *The* Rig Veda*: An Anthology*. London: Penguin, 1981.

Douglass, Frederick. "Farewell to the British People: An Address Delivered in London, England, March 30, 1847." In *The Frederick Douglass Papers: Series One—Speeches, Debates, and Interviews*, vol. 2, edited by John Blassingame et al. New Haven: Yale University Press, 1982.

———. *Narrative of the Life of Frederick Douglass, An American Slave*. Boston: Anti-Slavery Office, 1845.

Dowling, Mike. *Sergeant Rex: The Unbreakable Bond Between a Marine and His Military Working Dog*. New York: Atria Books, 2011.

Downey, Fairfax. *Dogs for Defense: American Dogs in the Second World War, 1941–45*. New York: Daniel P. McDonald, 1955.

Dumas, Charlotte. *Retrieved*. Los Angeles: The Ice Plant Publishers, 2011.

Ewers, Justin. "Dogs of War Get an Official 'Good Boy.'" *World War II* 22, no. 6 (2007): 12.

Fiedel, Stuart J. "Man's Best Friend—Mammoth's Worst Enemy? A Speculative Essay on the Role of Dogs in Paleoindian Colonization and Megafaunal Extinction." *World Archaeology* 37, no. 1 (2005): 11–25.

Fiegel, Amanda. "The Healing Power of Dogs." *National Geographic Daily News*. December 2012. http://news.nationalgeographic.co.uk/news/2012/12/121221-comfort-dogs-newtown-tragedy-animal-therapy/ (accessed April 15, 2013).

Fischer, Karen. "Training Sled Dogs at Camp Rimini: 1942–1944." *Montana: The Magazine of Western History* 34, no. 1 (1984): 10–19.

Flynn, Clifton. *Social Creatures: A Human-Animal Studies Reader*. New York: Lantern Books, 2008.

Forer, Ben. "Osama Bin Laden Raid: Navy SEALs Brought Highly Trained Dog with Them into Compound." ABC World News, May 5, 2011. http://abcnews.go.com/US/osama-bin-laden-raid-navy-seals-military-dog/story?id=13535070.

Forster, E. S. "Dogs in Ancient Warfare." *Greece and Rome* 10, no. 30 (1941): 114–17.

Foucault, Michel. *Security, Territory, Population: Lectures at the College of France 1977–78*. New York: Palgrave, 2007.

Franklin, Jon. *The Wolf in the Parlor: The Eternal Connection Between Humans and Dogs*. New York: Henry Holt, 2009.

Friedmann, E., A. H. Katcher, J. J. Lynch, and S. A. Thomas. "Animal Companions and One Year Survival of Patients after Discharge from a Coronary Care Unit." *Public Health Reports* 95 (1980): 307–12.

Furstinger, Nancy. *Mastiffs*. Edina, Minn.: ADBO Publishing, 2006.

Gatto, Maria. "The Aswan Area at the Dawn of Egyptian History." *Egyptian Archaeology* 35 (2009): 12–15.

Geertz, Clifford. "Religion as a Cultural System." In *The Interpretation of Cultures: Selected Essays*, 87–125. New York: Basic Books, 1973.

Germonpré, Mietje, M. Láznicková-Galetová, and M. V. Sablin. "Palaeolithic Dog Skulls at the Gravettian Predmostí Site, the Czech Republic." *Journal of Archaeological Science* 39, no. 1 (2012): 184–202.

Germonpré, Mietje, M. V. Sablin, R. E. Stevens, R. E. Hedges, M. Hofreiter, M. Stiller, and V. R. Després. "Fossil Dogs and Wolves from Palaeolithic Sites in Belgium, the Ukraine and Russia: Osteometry, Ancient DNA and Stable Isotopes." *Journal of Archaeological Science* 36, no. 2 (2009): 473–90.

Gibson, McGuire. "Nippur, 1990: Gula, Goddess of Healing, and an Akkadian Tomb." *The Oriental Institute News and Notes* 125 (September/October 1990).

Gilbert, Sandra, and Susan Gubar. "Horror's Twin: Mary Shelley's Monstrous Eve." In *The Madwoman in the Attic: The Woman Writer and the Nineteenth-Century Literary Imagination*, 213–47. New Haven: Yale University Press, 1979.

Goodavage, Maria. *Soldier Dogs: The Untold Story of America's Canine Heroes*. New York: New American Library, 2013.

Gorant, Jim. *The Lost Dogs: Michael Vick's Dogs and Their Tale of Rescue and Redemption*. New York: Gotham, 2011.

Graslund, Anne-Sofie. "Dogs in Graves—a Question of Symbolism?" In *Proceedings of the Conference at the Swedish Institute in Rome, September 9–12, 2002*, edited by B. S. Frizell, 167–76. Rome: The Swedish Institute in Rome, 2004.

Gray, Peter, and Sharon Young. "Human-Pet Dynamics in Cross-Cultural Perspective." *Anthrozoos* 24, no. 1 (2011): 17–30.

Green, Miranda. *Animals in Celtic Life and Myth*. London: Routledge, 1992.

———. *Symbol and Image in Celtic Religious Art*. New York: Sterling Publishing, 1997.

Gross, Aaron. "The Question of the Creature: Animals, Theology and Levinas' Dog." In *Creaturely Theology: On God, Humans and Other Animals*, edited by Celia Dean-Drummond and David Clough, 121–37. London: SCM Press, 2009.

Hachi: A Dog's Tale. Sony Pictures, 2009.

Hall, P. L., and Z. Malpus. "Pets as Therapy: Effects on Social Interaction in Long-Stay Psychiatry." *British Journal of Nursing* 9, no. 21 (2000): 2220–25.

Halpern, Baruch. "The Canine Conundrum of Ashkelon: A Classical Connection?" In *The Archaeology of Jordan and Beyond*, edited by L. E. Stager, J. A. Greene, and M. D. Coogan, 133–44. Winona Lake, Ind.: Eisenbrauns, 2000.

Hammond, Kim. "Monsters of Modernity: Frankenstein and Modern Environmentalism." *Cultural Geographies* 11, no. 2 (2004): 181–98.

Haraway, Donna. *The Companion Species Manifesto: Dogs, People and Significant Otherness.* Chicago: Prickly Paradigm Press, 2003.

Harbolt, Tami. *Bridging the Bond: The Cultural Construction of the Shelter Pet.* West Layfayette, Ind.: Purdue University Press, 2002.

Harrington, Spencer P. M. "Human Footprints at Chauvet Cave." *Archaeology* 52, no. 5 (1999): 18.

Hart, B. L., and K. L. Powell. "Antibacterial Properties of Saliva: Role in Maternal Periparturient Grooming and in Licking Wounds." *Physiology & Behavior* 48, no. 3 (1990): 383–86.

"A Helping Hound." *Mental Health Practice* (May 2012): 4.

Hill, Erica. "The Contextual Analysis of Animal Interments and Ritual Practice in Southwest North America." *Kiva* 65, no. 4 (2000): 361–98.

Hill, J. D. "The Identification of Ritual Deposits of Animals: A General Perspective from a Specific Study of 'Special Animal Deposits' from the Southern English Iron Age." In *Ritual Treatment of Human and Animal Remains*, edited by Sue Anderson and Katherine Boyle, 17–32. Oxford: Oxbow Books, 1996.

Hilts, Carly. "Iron Age Olives and Pampered Pets." *Current Archaeology* (online publication). London, July 20, 2012.

Hobgood-Oster, Laura. *The Friends We Keep: Unleashing Christianity's Compassion for Animals.* Waco, Tex.: Baylor University Press, 2010.

———. *Holy Dogs and Asses: Animals in the Christian Tradition.* Urbana: University of Illinois Press, 2008.

Hotz, Mary E. *Literary Remains: Representations of Death and Burial in Victorian England.* Albany: State University of New York Press, 2009.

Homans, John. *What's a Dog For? The Surprising History, Science, Philosophy and Politics of Man's Best Friend.* London: Penguin: 2012.

Horowitz, Alexandra. *Inside of a Dog: What Dogs See, Smell, and Know.* New York: Scribner, 2009.

Howell, Philip. "A Place for the Animal Dead: Pets, Pet Cemeteries and Animal Ethics in Late Victorian Britain." *Ethics, Place and Environment* 5, no. 1 (2002): 5–22.

HSUS (Humane Society of the United States). *An Advocate's Guide to Stopping Puppy Mills.* http://www.humanesociety.org/assets/pdfs/pets/puppy_mills/advocate_guide.pdf.

Hull, Douglas. *Hounds and Hunting in Ancient Greece.* Chicago: University of Chicago Press, 1964.

Jackson, Dennis A. "The Iron Age Site at Twywell, Northamptonshire." *Northamptonshire Archaeological Journal* 10 (1975): 31–95.

Jamison, Wesley, Caspar Wenk, and James Parker. "Every Sparrow That Falls: Understanding Animals Rights Activism as Functional Religion." *Society & Animals* 8, no. 3 (2000): 305–30.

Jenkins, Frank. "The Role of the Dog in Romano-Gaulish Religion." *Latomus* (Janvier–Mars 1957): 60–76. Société d'Etudes Latines de Bruxelles.

Jennings, Dana. *What a Difference a Dog Makes: Big Lessons on Life, Love and Healing from a Small Pooch.* New York: Doubleday, 2010.

Johnson, Peter. "The Modern Cemetery: A Design for Life." *Social and Cultural Geography* 9, no. 7 (2008): 777–90.

Karunanithy, David. "War Dogs among the Early Irish." *History Ireland* 17, no. 5 (2009): 16–19.

Katz, Jon. *The New Work of Dogs: Tending to Life, Love and Family.* New York: Random House, 2004.

Kelly, Kate. "The Government Asked for Pets for Defense in 1940s." *Huffington Post,* posted August 3, 2011. http://www.huffington post.com/kate-kelly/dogs-world-war-2_b_916760.html (accessed August 7, 2013).

Kercsmar, Joshua A. "Canine Evolution and the 'Improvement' of Nature in British America, ca. 1600–1800." Unpublished paper, presented at the American Historical Association Annual Meeting, Winter 2013.

Kete, Kathleen. *The Best in the Boudoir: Petkeeping in Nineteenth-Century Paris.* Berkeley: University of California Press, 1994.

King, Martin Luther, Jr. "Letter from Birmingham Jail." In *Liberating Faith: Religious Voices for Justice, Peace and Ecological Wisdom,* edited by R. Gottlieb, 177–87. Rowman & Littlefield, 2003.

Klose, Mychelle. *English Mastiffs.* Bloomington, Ind.: Booktango, 2012.

Koenig-Briker, Woodeene. *365 Saints: Your Daily Guide to the Wisdom and Wonder of Their Lives.* San Francisco: Harper, 1995.

Kryukova, Victoria. "Death as Defilement in Zoroastrianism." In *New Perspectives on Myth: Proceedings of the Second Annual Conference of the International Association for Comparative*

Mythology, edited by Wim van Binsbergen and Eric Venbrux, 75–90. Haarlem: Shikanda, 2010.

Kwong, Marilyn, and Kim Bartholomew. "Not Just a Dog: An Attachment Perspective on Relationships with Assistance Dogs." *Attachment & Human Development* 13, no. 5 (2011): 421–36.

Lanting, Fred. "Dogs in the Civil War." *TheDogPress*, June 2012. http://www.thedogpress.com/SideEffects/Civil-War-Dogs _Lanting-126.asp.

Lapham, Heather. "A Baumer Phase Dog Burial from the Kincaid Site in Southern Illinois." *Illinois Archaeology Survey* 22, no. 2 (2010): 437–63.

Larson, Greger, E. K. Karlsson, A. Perria, M. T. Webster, S. Y. W. Hoe, J. Peters, P. W. Stahl, et al. "Rethinking Dog Domestication by Integrating Genetics, Archeology, and Biogeography." *PNAS (Proceedings of the National Academy of Sciences) Early Edition*, May 21, 2012. http://www.pnas.org/content/ early/2012/05/15/1203005109.

Las Casas, Bartolomé de. *The Devastation of the Indies: A Brief Account*. Translated by H. Briffault. Baltimore: Johns Hopkins University Press, 1992.

Lemish, Michael. *War Dogs: A History of Loyalty and Heroism*. Dulles, Va.: Potomac Books, 1999.

Leroy, Grégoire, and R. Baumung. "Mating Practices and the Dissemination of Genetic Disorders in Domestic Animals, Based on the Example of Dog Breeding." *Animal Genetics* 42, no. 1 (2011): 66–74.

Leroy, Grégoire, and Xavier Rognon. "Assessing the Impact of Breeding Strategies on Inherited Disorders and Genetic Diversity in Dogs." *Veterinary Journal* 194, no. 3 (2012): 343–48.

Levinas, Emmanuel. "The Name of a Dog, or Natural Rights." In *Difficult Freedom: Essays in Judaism*. Translated by Sean Hand. Baltimore: Johns Hopkins University Press, 1990.

Lobell, Jarett, and Eric Powell. "Dogs of Roman Britain." *Archaeology Archive* 63:5 (2010). Published online at http://archive .archaeology.org/1009/dogs/romanbrits.html (last accessed September 16, 2013).

———. "More Than Man's Best Friend." *Archaeology* 63, no. 5 (2010). Published in *Archaeology Archive* online. http://archive. archaeology.org/1009/dogs/

Long, David. *Animal Heroes: Inspiring True Stories of Courageous Animals*. New York: Random House, 2013.

Lorenz, Konrad. *King Solomon's Ring*. New York: Plume, 1997.

————. *Man Meets Dog*. New York: Routledge, 2002.

Lowry, Aislinn. "Sexual Healing: Gender and Sexuality in the Healing Cult of Asklepios." Illinois Wesleyan University Honors Projects. Paper #4, 2010. http://digitalcommons.iwu.edu/grs_honproj/4.

Lupo, Karen, and Joel Janetski. "Evidence of the Domesticated Dogs and Some Related Canids in the Eastern Great Basin." *Journal of California and Great Basin* 16, no. 2 (1994): 199–220.

Lycophron. *Alexandra*. Translated by A. W. Mair. Loeb Classical Library 129. New York: Putnam, 1921.

Mackail, John W. *Select Epigrams from the Greek Anthology*. Charleston, S.C.: BiblioBazaar, 2008.

MacKinnon, Michael, and Kyle Belanger. "In Sickness and in Health: Care for an Arthritic Maltese Dog from the Roman Cemetery of Yasmina, Carthage, Tunisia." In *Dogs and People in Social, Working, Economic or Symbolic Interaction*, edited by L. M. Snyder and E. A. Moore, 38–43. Oxford: Oxbow Books, 2007.

Manaserian, N. H., and L. Antonian. "Dogs of Armenia." In Crockford, *Dogs Through Time*, 227–35.

Mazzorin, Jacopo De Grossi, and Antonio Tagliacozzo. "Morphological and Osteological Changes in the Dog from the Neolithic to the Roman Period in Italy." In Crockford, *Dogs Through Time*, 141–61.

McBrien, Richard. *Lives of the Saints*. San Francisco: HarperSanFrancisco, 2001.

McCulloch, Michael, Tadeusz Jezierski, Michael Broffman, Alan Hubbard, Kirk Turner, and Teresa Janecki. "Diagnostic Accuracy of Canine Scent Detection in Early- and Late-Stage Lung and Breast Cancers." *Integrative Cancer Therapies* 5, no. 1 (2006): 30–39.

McHann, Marjorie. *My Rescued Golden: True Stories of Rescued Golden Retrievers and the People Who Love Them*. Lincoln, Neb.: iUniverse, 2002.

Meadows, A. J. *Hurricane Katrina Animal Rescue: A Story Buried Deep*. Victoria, Canada: Friesen Press, 2011.

Mellor, Anne. *Mary Shelley: Her Life, Her Fiction, Her Monsters*. New York: Routledge, 1988.

Miklósi, Ádám. *Dog: Behaviour, Evolution, and Cognition*. Oxford: Oxford University Press, 2007.

Montague, J. "Continuing Care—Back to the Garden." *Hospitals & Health Networks* 69, no. 17 (1995): 58–60.

Morey, Darcy. *Dogs: Domestication and the Development of a Social Bond.* Cambridge: Cambridge University Press, 2010.

Morley, John. *Death and the Victorians.* London: Studio Vista, 1971.

Morris, Patricia. "Managing Pet Owners' Guilt and Grief in Veterinary Euthanasia Encounters." *Journal of Contemporary Ethnography* 41, no. 3 (2012): 337–65.

Murphy, Claire Rudolph, and Jane G. Haigh. *Gold Rush Dogs.* Anchorage: Alaska Northwest Books, 2001.

Musil, Rudolf. "Evidence for the Domestication of Wolves in Central European Magdalenian Sites." In Crockford, *Dogs Through Time,* 21–28.

Napierala, Hannes, and Hans-Peter Uerpmann. "A 'New' Paleolithic Dog from Central Europe." *International Journal of Osteoarchaeology* 22, no. 2 (2012): 127–37.

Nasser, Dave. *Giant George: Life with the World's Biggest Dog.* New York: Grand Central Life and Style, 2012.

National Canine Research Council. "The Problems with Dog Bite Studies." Updated January 28, 2013. Amenia, N.Y.: NCRC.

National Institutes of Health. "Variants in Three Genes Account for Most Dog Coat Differences." *NIH News,* August 27, 2009. http://www.nih.gov/news/health/aug2009/nhgri-27.htm (accessed August 11, 2013).

Neal, Andrea. "Trained Dogs Transforming Lives." *Saturday Evening Post,* September 1, 2005: 64–66.

Nicholson, Paul T. "Dogs as Food." *Archaeology* 63, no. 5 (2010). Published in *Archaeology Archive* online. http://archive.archaeology.org/1009/dogs/catacomb.html.

———. "The Saqqara Dog Catacombs." Cardiff University website, http://www.cardiff.ac.uk/hisar/people/pn/e_dogs.html (accessed September 2013).

Nonnus. *Dionysiaca.* Book 3. Edited by W. H. D. Rouse et al. Cambridge, Mass.: Harvard University Press, 1940.

Olmert, Meg Daley. *Made for Each Other: the Biology of the Human-Animal Bond.* Boston: Merloyd Lawrence, 2009.

Olsen, Sandra. "The Secular and Sacred Roles of Dogs at North Kazakhstan." In Crockford, *Dogs Through Time,* 71–92.

Oppenheimer, Mark. "Churches Take Steps to Show Their Love for Animals." *New York Times.* http://www.nytimes.com/2011/10/15/us/pet-ministries-are-growing-in-churches.html?_r=0.

Ornan, Tallay. "The Goddess Gula and Her Dog." *Israel Museum Studies in Archaeology* 3 (2004): 13–30.

Ovodov, Nikolai D., Susan J. Crockford, Yaroslav V. Kuzmin,

Thomas F. G. Higham, Gregory W. L. Hodgins, and Johannes van der Plicht. "A 33,000-Year-Old Incipient Dog from the Altai Mountains of Siberia: Evidence of the Earliest Domestication Disrupted by the Last Glacial Maximum." *PLOS ONE: The Paleontology Collection* 6, no. 7 (2011): 1–7.

Page, Jake. *Do Dogs Laugh?* New York: HarperCollins, 2007 (previously published as *Dogs: A Natural History*).

Palagruto, Anne. *Civil War Dogs and the Men Who Loved Them.* Seattle: CreateSpace Independent Publishing Platform, 2008.

Pappas, Stephanie. "Starchy Diets May Have Given Ancient Dogs a Paw Up." LiveScience. January 23, 2013. http://www.livescience.com/26513-starchy-human-diet-domesticated-dogs.html.

Patrick (Saint). *Confession (St. Patrick's Confessio).* Online version available in English translation at http://www.confessio.ie/etexts/confessio_english#01.

Pennisi, Elizabeth. "Diet Shaped Dog Domestication." Sciencemag.org. January 23, 2013. http://news.sciencemag.org/sciencenow/2013/01/dog-domestication-tied-to-starch.html.

Pickeral, Tamsin. *The Dog: 5000 Years of the Dog in Art.* London: Merrell, 2008.

Pionnier-Capitan, M., C. Bemilli, P. Bodu, G. Célérier, J.-G. Ferrié, P. Fosse, M. Garcià, and J.-D. Vigne. "New Evidence for Upper Palaeolithic Small Domestic Dogs in South-Western Europe." *Journal of Archaeological Science* 38, no. 9 (2011): 2123–40.

Plumb, John H. *The Commercialisation of Leisure in Eighteenth-Century England.* Reading: University of Reading Press, 1973.

Plutarch. *Plutarch's Lives*, vol. 3. Seattle: CreateSpace Independent Publishing Platform, 2008.

Pollan, Michael. *The Botany of Desire: A Plant's-Eye View of the World.* New York: Random House, 2001.

Polyaenus. *Stratagems of War.* Translated by P. Krentz and E. Wheeler. Chicago: Ares Publishing, 1994.

Preece, Rod. *Awe for the Tiger, Love for the Lamb: A Chronicle of Sensibility to Animals.* Vancouver: University of British Columbia Press, 2002.

Raisor, Michelle. *Determining the Antiquity of Dog Origins: Canine Domestication as a Model for the Consilience between Molecular Genetics and Archaeology.* Ph.D. Diss., Texas A&M University. August 2004.

Reisner, George. "The Dog Which Was Honored by the King of Upper and Lower Egypt." *Bulletin of the Museum of Fine Arts, Boston* 34, no. 206 (1936): 96–99.

Ritvo, Harriet. *The Animal Estate: The English and Other Creatures in the Victorian Age*. Cambridge, Mass.: Harvard University Press, 1987.

Rogak, Lisa. *The Dogs of War: The Courage, Love and Loyalty of Military Working Dogs*. New York: St. Martin's Griffin, 2011.

Roth, Melinda. *The Man Who Talks to Dogs*. New York: St. Martin's Griffin, 2004.

Rowan, Andrew, and Alan Beck. "The Health Benefits of Human-Animal Interactions." In *Social Creatures: A Human and Animal Studies Reader*, edited by C. Flynn, 275–80. Seattle: Lantern Books, 2008.

Ruark, Robert, Lt. (USNR). "Have the War Dogs Been Good Soldiers?" *Saturday Evening Post*, November 25, 1944, 11–12, 93.

Russell, Edmund. *Evolutionary History: Uniting History and Biology to Understand Life on Earth*. Cambridge: Cambridge University Press, 2011.

Russell, Nerissa. *Social Zooarchaeology: Humans and Animals in Prehistory*. Cambridge: Cambridge University Press, 2012.

Sablin, Mikhail, and Gennady Khlopachev. "The Earliest Ice Age Dogs: Evidence from Eliseevichi I." *Current Anthropology* 43, no. 7 (2002): 795–99.

Saunders, Jeffrey, and Edward Daeschler. "Descriptive Analyses and Taphonomical Observations of Culturally-Modified Mammoths Excavated at 'The Gravel Pit,' Near Clovis, New Mexico in 1936." *Proceedings of the Academy of Natural Sciences of Philadelphia* 145 (1994): 1–28.

Savolainen, Peter, Ya-ping Zhang, Jing Luo, Joakim Lundeberg, and Thomas Leitner. "Genetic Evidence for an East Asian Origin of Domestic Dogs." *Science* 298, no. 5598 (2002): 1610–13.

Schwartz, Marion. *A History of Dogs in the Early Americas*. New Haven: Yale University Press, 1998.

"Scientists Unlock the Mystery Surrounding a Tale of Shaggy Dogs." *ScienceDaily*, November 27, 2011. http://www.sciencedaily.com/releases/2011/11/111124150355.htm (accessed August 8, 2013).

Scott, Cathy. *Pawprints of Katrina: Pets Saved and Lessons Learned*. Hoboken, N.J.: Howell Book House, 2008.

Serpell, James, ed. *The Domestic Dog: Its Evolution, Behaviour and Interactions with People*. Cambridge: Cambridge University Press, 1995.

———. "From Paragon to Pariah: Some Reflections on Human Attitudes to Dogs." In Serpell, *The Domestic Dog*, 246–56.

Shearman, Jeremy, and Alan Wilton. "Origins of the Domestic Dog and the Rich Potential for Gene Mapping." *Genetic Research International* (2011): 1–6.

Shelley, Mary. *Frankenstein; or, The Modern Prometheus*, edited by Johanna M. Smith. 2nd ed. Boston: Bedford, 2000.

Shigehara, Nobuo, and Hitomi Hongo. "Ancient Remains of Jomon Dogs from Neolithic Sites in Japan." In Crockford, *Dogs Through Time*, 61–67.

Shushan, Gregory. "Afterlife Conceptions in the Vedas." *Religion Compass 5*, no. 6 (2011): 202–13.

Sims, Joseph Patterson. *"A Dog Map of the World": The Countries of Origin of Some Seventy Breeds of Domesticated Dogs, Half of Them Evolved in the British Isles!* London: Illustrated London News, 1933.

Skabelund, Aaron. *Empire of Dogs: Canines, Japan and the Making of the Modern Imperial World*. Ithaca, N.Y.: Cornell University Press, 2011.

Smith, Johanna M. " 'Cooped Up' with 'Sad Trash': Domesticity and the Sciences in *Frankenstein*." In *Frankenstein; or, The Modern Prometheus*, edited by Johanna M. Smith, 314–31. 2nd ed. Boston: Bedford, 2000.

Smith, Kate. "Guides, Guards and Gifts to the Gods: Domesticated Dogs in the Art and Archaeology of Iron Age and Roman Britain." Oxford: Archaeopress, 2006.

Smyth, Claire, and Eamonn Slevin. "Experiences of Family Life with an Autism Assistance Dog." *Learning Disability Practice 13*, no. 4 (2010): 12–17.

Stager, Lawrence. "Why Were Hundreds of Dogs Buried at Ashkelon?" *Biblical Archaeology Review 17*, no. 3 (1991): 26–39.

Stanford, Dennis. "Bison Kill by Ice Age Hunters." *National Geographic 155*, no. 1 (1979): 114–21.

Strange, Julie-Marie. " 'Tho' Lost to Sight, to Memory Dear': Pragmatism, Sentimentality and Working-Class Attitudes towards the Grave, c. 1875–1914." *Mortality 8*, no. 2 (2003): 144–59.

Strelan, Rick. *Paul, Artemis and the Jews in Ephesus*. Berlin: de Gruyter, 1996.

Stone, Ken. "The Dogs of Exodus and the Question of the Animal." Paper presented at "Divinanimality: Creaturely Theology." Conference, Drew Theological Seminary, October 2011.

Sutter, Nathan, and Elaine Ostrander. "Dog Star Rising: The Canine Genetic System." *Nature Reviews Genetics 5*, no. 12 (2004): 900–910.

Tchernov, Eitan. "Two New Dogs, and Other Natufian Dogs, from the Southern Levant." *Journal of Archaeological Science* 24, no. 1 (1997): 65–95.

Thurston, M. Elizabeth. *The Lost History of the Canine Race.* Kansas City: Andrews & McMeel, 1996.

Torben, Rick, Phillip Walker, Lauren Willis, Anna Noah, Jon Erlandson, Rene Vellanoweth, Todd Braje, and Douglas Kennett. "Dogs, Humans and Island Ecosystems: The Distribution, Antiquity and Ecology of Domestic Dogs on California's Channel Islands, USA." *The Holocene* 18, no. 7 (2008): 1077–87.

Townshend, Emma. *Darwin's Dogs: How Darwin's Pets Helped Form a World-Changing Theory of Evolution.* London: Frances Lincoln, 2009.

Trut, Lyudmila N. "Early Canid Domestication: The Farm-Fox Experiment." *American Scientist* 87, no. 2 (1999): 160–69.

Tsouparopoulou, Christina. "The 'K-9 Corps' of the Third Dynasty of Ur: The Dog Handlers at Drehem and the Army." *Zeitschrift für Assyriologie und vorderasiatische Archäologie* 102, no. 1 (2012): 1–16.

Turner, Pamela. *Hachiko Waits: The True Story of a Loyal Dog.* New York: Houghton Mifflin, 2004.

Turton, Douglas. "The Virtual Pet Cemetery—Internet World Pavilion." *Implicit Religion* 11, no. 3 (2008): 313–15.

Tushaus, Katherine. "Don't Buy the Doggy in the Window: Ending the Cycle That Perpetuates Commercial Breeding with Regulation of the Retail Pet Industry." *Drake Journal of Agricultural Law* 14, no. 3 (2009): 501–19.

Twining, Hillary, Arnold Arluke, and Gary Patronek. "Managing the Stigma of Outlaw Breeds: A Case Study of Pit Bull Owners." *Society and Animals* 8, no. 1 (2000): 1–28.

Tyson, Peter. "Dogs' Dazzling Sense of Smell." *NOVA Science Now*, online PBS journal, posted October 4, 2012. http://www.pbs .org/wgbh/nova/nature/dogs-sense-of-smell.html last (accessed August 6, 2013).

Valensi, Patricia. "The Archaeozoology of Lazaret Cave." *International Journal of Osteoarchaeology* 10, no. 5 (2000): 357–67.

Varley, Edwin. *Judy Story: The Dog with Six Lives.* London: Souvenir Press, 1976.

Vick, Michael. *Finally Free: An Autobiography.* Brentwood, Tenn.: Worthy Publishing, 2012.

Vigne, Jean-Denis. "L'humérus de chien magdalénien de Erralla (Gipuzkoa, Espagne) et la domestication tardiglaciaire du loup en Europe." *Munibe Antropologia-Arkeologia* 57 (2005): 279–87.

Vila, C., J. E. Maldonado, and R. K. Wayne. "Phylogenetic Relationships, Evolution, and Genetic Diversity of the Domestic Dog." *Journal of Heredity* 90, no. 1 (1999): 71–77.

Vilà, C., P. Savolainen, J. E. Maldonado, I. R. Amorim, J. E. Rice, R. L. Honeycutt, K. A. Crandall, J. Lundeberg, and R. K. Wayne. "Multiple and Ancient Origins of the Domestic Dog." *Science* 276, no. 5319 (1997): 1687–89.

von Holdt, Bridgett M., John P. Pollinger, Kirk E. Lohmueller, Eunjung Han, Heidi G. Parker, Pascale Quignon, Jeremiah D. Degenhardt, et al. "Genome-Wide SNP and Haplotype Analyses Reveal a Rich History Underlying Dog Domestication." *Nature* 464 (2010): 898–902.

Walton, Alice. *The Cult of Asklepios.* Cornell Studies in Classical Philology 3. Boston: Ginn, 1894.

Walton, John K. "Mad Dogs and Englishmen: The Conflict over Rabies in Late Victorian England." *Journal of Social History* 13, no. 2 (1979): 219–39.

Wang, Jessica. "Dogs and the Making of the American State: Voluntary Association, State Power, and the Politics of Animal Control in New York City, 1850–1920." *Journal of American History* 98, no. 4 (2012): 998–1024.

Wapnish, P., and B. Hesse. "Pampered Pooches or Plain Pariahs? The Ashkelon Dog Burials." *Biblical Archaeologist* 56, no. 2 (1993): 55–80.

Warren, Diane. "Palaeopathology of Archaic Period Dogs from the North American Southeast." In Crockford, *Dogs Through Time*, 105–10.

Wayne, R. K. "Molecular Evolution of the Dog Family." *Trends in Genetics* 9, no. 6 (1993): 218–24.

Webb, Stephen. *On God and Dogs: A Christian Theology of Compassion for Animals.* Oxford: Oxford University Press, 1998.

Wegner, Josef. "Beneath the Mountain-of-Anubis: Ancient Egypt's First Hidden Royal Tomb." *Expedition* 48, no. 2 (2006): 15–19.

Werner, Louis. "Dog Tails of the New World." *Americas* 51, no. 5 (1999): 40–48.

White, David. *Myths of the Dog-Man.* Chicago: University of Chicago Press, 1991.

Williams, Laurie. *Just Gus: A Rescued Dog and the Woman He Loved.* New York: McWitty Press, 2005.

Wilson, Cindy C., and Dennis C. Turner, eds. *Companion Animals in Human Health.* Thousand Oaks, Calif.: Sage: 1997.

Wordsworth, William. *Wordsworth: Complete Poetical Works.* Compiled and edited by Ernest de Selincourt and Thomas Hutchinson. London: Oxford University Press, 1961.

Wozencraft, W. C. "Carnivora: Canidae." In *Mammal Species of the World: A Taxonomic and Geographic Reference,* edited by D. E. Wilson and D. M. Reeder, 279–88. Baltimore, Md.: Johns Hopkins University Press, 2005.

Wroe, Stephen, Judith Field, Richard Fullagar, and Lars S. Jermin. "Megafaunal Extinction in the Late Quaternary and the Global Overkill Hypothesis." *Alcheringa: An Australasian Journal of Palaeontology* 28, no. 1 (2004): 291–331.

Yohe, Robert, and Max Pavesic. "Early Archaic Domestic Dogs from Western Idaho, USA." In Crockford, *Dogs Through Time,* 93–104.

Young, Julie K., Kirk A. Olson, Richard P. Reading, Sukh Amgalanbaatar, and Joel Berger. "Is Wildlife Going to the Dogs? Impacts of Feral and Free-roaming Dogs on Wildlife Populations." *BioScience* 61, no. 2 (2011): 125–32.

Yuhong, Wu. "Rabies and Rabid Dogs in Sumerian and Akkadian Literature." *Journal of the American Oriental Society* 121, no. 1 (2001): 32–43.

Zucchero, Michael. *Loyal Hearts: Histories of Civil War Canines.* Lynchburg, Va.: Schroeder Publications, 2009.

Index

aboriginal dog, 29, 154n39;
  dingo, 28, 31, 154n39;
  Eskimo, 29, 96; Inca, 96;
  Klamath Indian, 96; Mexican
  hairless, 29, 96, 112, 145n66;
  Plains Indian, 29, 96
Achilles, 51
Andamanese (Bay of Bengal), 31
Africa, 9, 17, 27, 27, 97, 100,
  108, 109, 141n16, 144n54,
  155n43; *see also* Egypt
afterlife, 3–4, 33–59, 77, 83,
  129, 148n46; Ashkelon, 43;
  Egypt, 40–42; guides to, 49,
  130; Japan, 47; Peru, 48;
  "Rainbow Bridge, The," 57;
  rituals, 51; Victorian period,
  36, 146n7
agriculture, 2, 19, 20, 26–28,
  116, 140n11
Alaska, 38
Alexander the Great, 44, 83–84,
  94, 147n29; Peritas (dog), 44,
  83–84, 147n29

American Kennel Club, 116,
  157n28
American Society for the Prevention of Cruelty to Animals, 38,
  157n23
Antarctica, 41
anthropogenic environments, 8,
  18, 144n54
Anubis, 42, 51–52, 148n50
Arctic, 3, 8; search and rescue
  units, World War II, 88–89;
  wolves, 18
Armenia, 27, 29, 65, 144n58,
  145n63, 150n21
art: Bayeux Tapestry, 85; caves,
  in, 6; "Cave Canem," 82; dogs
  in, 7, 53–54, 144n57, 149n57,
  153n10; Glasgow School
  of Art, 73; Metropolitan
  Museum of Art, New York,
  144n57; rock art, 26–27; Tutankhamun chest, 82–83
Artemis, 26, 151n25, 151n26
Ashkelon (modern-day Israel),

179